An Education in Service Management

A guide to building a successful service management career and delivering organisational success

An Education in Service Management

A guide to building a successful service management career and delivering organisational success

DAVID BARROW
CITP FBCS

IT Governance Publishing

IT Governance Publishing Ltd
Unit 3, Clive Court
Bartholomew's Walk
Cambridgeshire Business Park
Ely, Cambridgeshire
CB7 4EA
United Kingdom
www.itgovernancepublishing.co.uk

First edition published in the United Kingdom in 2023 by IT Governance Publishing

ISBN 978-1-78778-561-8 (hc.)
ISBN 978-1-78778-467-3 (pb.)

DEDICATION

To my mum. This one's for you.

RIP.

ABOUT THE AUTHOR

"At sixteen, I fluked my way into information technology during an interview assessment day."

"I've remained in information technology due to a genuine desire to innovate as a technologist. I work in 'service' due to a passion for co-creating value, which has driven me from my days as a service desk analyst to the present day as an enterprise service management consultant, speaker and author."

David Barrow: November 2023

David's career has taken him into various industries, including IBM Global Services, (now known as IBM Global Business Services), where he first began working in information technology service management.

In 1999, David authored "Enterprise Service Management" processes for IBM Service Desks. Here, he discovered IT as a service and set a path to deliver IT services that were as valuable as they were functional.

David was introduced to ITIL® as part of his work at IBM. He has taken a journey that follows ITIL from v2 to the current version, with certification as an ITIL Master & VeriSM Professional among his achievements.

The Chartered Institute for Information Technology (the BCS), recognises David as a Chartered Information Technology Professional, awarding him a fellowship of the BCS in 2022.

David is passionate about service management, acting as a subject matter expert with EXIN and the International Foundation for Digital Competences (IFDC), presenting to global C-level audiences on the '10 steps to digital transformation'. He has also been a panellist on the 'ITSM Crowd', and the 'Service Management Leadership' and 'Enterprise Digital' podcasts, where the discussions centred around enterprise service management and its future as an organisational enabler.

David is a committee member for IT service management (ITSM) on behalf of the British Standards Institute (BSI), the BCS and the International Organization for Standardization (ISO).

David hosts his own YouTube channel titled "IT's all about Choices", which focuses on building careers within IT and invites guests from different backgrounds and professions to discuss how IT and choices have formed their careers and belief systems.

David's passion for service management extends to helping people and organisations make a success of themselves. He acts as a mentor to people at various levels both in partnership with Reed within the Women in Technology programme and the British Computer Society, hence his desire to put together this book in the hope that it helps you, the reader, to develop a greater understanding of service management and its ability to deliver fantastic success for your organisation, those who work with you and ultimately for you as you develop your own career.

FOREWORDS

David is a student and teacher with unique insights into IT and, specifically, the human side of IT, making his work profoundly valuable!

On a more personal note, David is one of my students and also one of my teachers – as it should be!

It is, therefore, not a surprise to me that this work once again showcases how David adds value to his customers and industry at large.

Service management is seemingly at a crossroads, and many question the value of the discipline in an age of Agile and DevOps and all things new.

Does service management not belong to an illustrious past? Does it have any relevance here and now? Or are we desperately clinging to something that is best left in the past?

As usual, David provides a unique perspective on the above questions and 'insightful insights' to those who would argue that it is not worth reading yet another book on service management.

His journey and insights will also serve as a valuable reference for you, as you struggle to find answers. The answers may not always be what you wanted to hear, but in typical David Barrow style, they are good answers you need to hear.

In this book, David provides us with new insights (and old context) into IT and enterprise service management!

Johann Botha – Johannesburg, April 2023

Forewords

When I spoke to David about his book *An Education in Service Management*, the title appealed to me as I consider myself an educator in IT service management and I was keen to understand what he meant.

Being educated in service management is not just about acquiring knowledge of the processes and practices, but about developing attitudes and nurturing behaviours. This must include the cultural aspects (and norms) that underpin how we do things. Essentially, it is 'gearing up' people to work and progress in a career in service management in general, as well as acknowledging the challenges posed to those aspiring to a career in IT. Importantly, ***an education*** is necessary to those already working in it.

The book also touches on a new dimension: building awareness of the principles and opportunities service management brings to a multitude of management positions within an organisation. This is very important because we live and work in a predominantly service economy. Current figures show that all economies are becoming more reliant on services as they play a key role in their country's gross domestic product (GDP). In developed economies, the figure is 80% plus. In middle- and low-income economies, the figures are 60% and 50% respectively, and the dependency on all economies rises each year. According to OECD analysis, in high-income economies the impact on employment is about 90%.

The development of sophisticated technologies has played a crucial role in the emergence of the service economy and servitisation. Together, this created a flurry of activity in the 1980s by those working in the technology environment to quickly devise a set of best practices geared to the management of IT. The rush to deliver the best practices to existing technology professionals created a 'training environment', built on quick delivery; accreditation came later. This was understandable, and was certainly relevant at the time, but questions remain about the viability of this being the primary learning model today and whether new approaches are necessary.

Most services are facilitated, enabled and driven by technology. The successful deployment of services requires touchpoints across broader management theories and disciplines. Co-creating value across the organisation is one such fundamental concept, which has long been spoken about in management circles but is now recognised as being just as important when technology is involved. By adopting a broader set of management techniques, they should not be seen as dry or cerebral concepts, but active and practical mechanisms to respond to today's challenges and opportunities.

David has a longstanding record of working in computing and management environments, and as such acknowledges the main encounters of working in the service industry. He also understands that knowledge-sharing, engagement across the organisation and the need for practical awareness are essential. Importantly, he stresses the need to develop a community of practice to support a wide audience that encompasses both technology and management professionals.

David's style and approach throughout the book is built on his discussions with senior managers from a range of industries. He embeds this in the book to encourage those from other parts of the organisation to engage with IT service management ideas and knowledge.

Correspondingly, it was pleasing to see observations from professionals working in service management woven into the theme of the book. There is a common thread within those comments that echo my experiences of someone who has worked in IT, but also taught IT as a service to students. They recognise that there is a gap in the way we understand the core knowledge and that there is a need for a wider set of skills that are necessary in the workplace. David has spotted this too and addresses it in the book.

Regarding mainstream education, it can be observed that computing as a subject is popular with a certain student mindset; similarly with management. They are sometimes seen as two separate disciplines that are poles apart from each other and generally built upon established research traditions. According to current information, there are only a smattering of university courses that include 'industry standard' IT service management best-practice material. Thus, students can be in a 'pot luck' situation as to what they learn about the subject in their institution. In the UK, there are swathes of IT and business graduates who are likely to know very little about the core concepts of managing IT as a service. It may well be there are similar experiences worldwide.

Since IT service management training has predominated the market since the beginning, there are entrenched issues about the way mainstream education can become more involved in learning. There is the cost of examination accreditation, the general lack of experience and knowledge of academics, and questions about how best to design specific courses. This means that there is unlikely to be consistent integration into mainstream education for some time.

For students, the inability to acquire core knowledge from college or university and a lack of a multidisciplinary approach to learning are problematic for young people entering the workforce. There is also the added complexity of an emerging set of service management techniques that can create a vacuum of knowledge and understanding across all parts of the organisation.

David has also identified that these are two important and complementary issues: the lack of awareness of IT service management at board level and the lack of knowledge of young professionals. Through this unique understanding, he has been able to put forward some engaging and inspiring ideas. He writes in a down-to-earth style and puts forward sensible courses of action with a pragmatism constructed upon ideas and thoughts gleaned from his real-life working experiences.

The underlying narrative in the book is built upon storytelling, which is sure to please multiple audiences as they seek to walk on a pathway in their organisation. It will also be especially important for those starting a career in technology.

Sandra Whittleston
MA (Ed), BSc (Hons) Computing, FHEA
Open University
July 2023

References and further reading:

- Buckley P, Majumdar R (2018). Deloitte Insights "The Services Powerhouse: Increasingly vital to world economic growth", *https://www2.deloitte.com/us/en/insights/economy/issues-by-the-numbers/trade-in-services-economy-growth.html*.
- Buera FJ, Kaboski JP (2009). "The rise of the service economy": Cambridge MA, National Bureau of Economic Research.
- GOV UK (2023). "Service Industries: Key Economic Indicators Research Briefing", *https://commonslibrary.parliament.uk/research-briefings/sn02786/*.
- OECD (2019). "Contributions to business sector services' productivity", in OECD Compendium of Productivity Indicators 2019, OECD Publishing, Paris. DOI: *https://doi.org/10.1787/7a09d39c-en*.
- OECD (2021). "OECD Economic Outlook, Volume 2021 Issue 2" OECD Publishing, Paris, *https://doi-org.libezproxy.open.ac.uk/10.1787/66c5ac2c-en*.
- Pollard C (2010). "Global Issues in IT Servitization and IT Service Management" Journal of Global Information Technology Management 1-7-2010, Vol 13 (4) pgs 1-3.

CONTRIBUTORS

This book will discuss how we can co-create all that is good in ITSM and make it more enterprise-focused. It will do so by exploring those ingredients that make good enterprise-focused service management professionals and discussing what makes service management valuable as an enterprise function.

Over the years, David has been privileged to have some fantastic managers, colleagues, customers and mentors. One element that makes these people unique is their agreement to contribute to this publication.

His heartfelt thanks go out to you all:

- **Suzanne D. Van Hove, Ed.D.:**
  Dr Suzanne D. Van Hove has successfully blended an award-winning career in higher education with a passion for service management. As a lead author for *VeriSM: A Service Management Approach for the Digital Age* and *VeriSM: Unwrapped and Applied*, she continues to push the development of service management across the entire organisation as well as advocating a hybrid approach to service delivery.
  Suzanne has published and collaborated on numerous articles, blogs and videos. She represents the US within the international standards community and is the convenor for JTC1/SC40 Working Group 2, *Service Management – Information Technology*. Suzanne is a frequent lecturer in various universities

worldwide, delivering service management concepts to IS/IT/MBA students. In 2013, she was presented with the itSMF USA Lifetime Achievement in Service Management award and named a Top 25 Thought Leader by HDI.

- **Claire Agutter:**
  Claire Agutter is a service management trainer, consultant and author with over two decades of experience. She founded ITSM Zone, providing accredited elearning and is the director of Scopism, and is a co-author on the SIAM Foundation and SIAM Professional books.[1]
  In 2018–23, *Computer Weekly* nominated her as one of the most influential women in technology. Claire hosts the popular ITSM Crowd YouTube channel and is the chief architect for VeriSM.
- **Doug Oram:**
  Doug Oram is an IT service management leader and consultant with over 30 years' experience.
  Doug's career in IT has included several international roles across IT operations, service delivery management

---

[1] For more information, visit: *https://www.itgovernancepublishing.co.uk/product/service-integration-and-management-siam-foundation-body-of-knowledge-bok-second-edition* and *https://www.itgovernancepublishing.co.uk/product/service-integration-and-management-siam-professional-body-of-knowledge-bok-second-edition*. Claire's author page can be found here: *https://www.itgovernancepublishing.co.uk/author/claire-agutter*.

and service introduction across finance, retail, education, government (including UK test and trace) and advertising/media. Being very astute, detail-oriented, customer-focused and a proponent of continual service improvement, Doug's forte is building strong working relationships across organisations at all levels.

- **Lucy Grimwade (she/her):**
  Lucy Grimwade has over 15 years' experience working in service management. She has worked in global teams and developed and implemented ITSM processes across multiple industries. Lucy's work is dedicated to identifying and applying improvements and ITSM change across people, processes and technology, enabling shifts in mindsets and delivering value that empowers business success.
- **Matt Robinson (he/him):**
  Matt Robinson started his service journey in retail and market stalls before landing an account manager job in his 20s.

  Matt didn't intend to end up in service management or IT. Still, as he gained experience in how better service delivery can lead to a better outcome, he fell in love with making service delivery matter. Matt is a champion of inclusion and of understanding how we can make IT and IT services work for everyone so that we get the best value for everyone.
- **Suzanne Galletly:**
  Suzanne Galletly started her career in service management before switching to the IT education

industry, where she has more than 17 years' experience. She is the portfolio director at EXIN, where she is accountable for developing and positioning EXIN's Digital Skills certification portfolio in line with market needs and industry trends. Suzanne is also chair of the International Foundation of Digital Competences (IFDC).

She is a regular speaker at international conferences on the topic of (digital) skills development and is a passionate advocate of lifelong learning.

- **Alex Conroy:**

  Alex Conroy has over 18 years' experience in IT recruitment. During this time, he has achieved certification in ITIL V3 and gained a sound knowledge of all stages of the recruitment life cycle, specialising in leading the recruitment at Reed Technology for IT service management roles.

- **Gareth Jones**:

  Gareth Jones is an experienced project manager with a background in business analysis, working on a consultancy basis since 2007. Gareth has extensive experience of scoping and delivering digital projects across multiple industries in the private and public sectors, including education, social care, charities, pharmaceutical, law and, more recently, travel loyalty and insurance.

- **Tracy Venter:**

  Tracy Venter is a service delivery management leader in a global enterprise with over 20 years' experience delivering excellent digital services for her customers. She has vast experience in creating, building and managing service management teams and leading global service delivery, engineering, project management and programme-led cross-functional teams, developing skills and productivity within those teams.

- **Sundeep Singh**:
  Sundeep Singh is a service strategy lead at the Co-op, focused on driving a modern service management transformation agenda across the technology function.
  Sundeep has over a decade of experience running service-focused teams, providing consultancy and technical support for ITSM tools, and implementing business-driven service management processes.
- **Daniel Breston:**
  Daniel Breston is a retired CIO and principle consultant that spent his career blending Agile, Lean, ITSM and DevOps principles into a way of leading teams and helping organisations benefit from technology. He now blogs occasionally or speaks at hosted events. Daniel is also a board member of itSMF UK.
- **Suraj Bithal:**
  Suraj Bithal is an interim C-level executive with over 20 years' experience in product development, infrastructure and enterprise service management.
  His passion is to lead and transform companies and enable business and technical transformation while creating high-performance teams. Frequently asked by boards and leaders to advise and drive change, Suraj

uses his experience leading global teams across various sectors to inspire senior executives to make decisions that will positively impact their business efficiencies, finances, productivity and, more importantly, their people.

Suraj inspires change and growth within organisations and the people around him with his energy and vision while developing culture, experience and ambition to change.

Suraj wants to positively impact IT, organisations, institutions, and the people they serve.

- **Simone Jo-Moore**:

  Simone Jo-Moore pushes the boundaries and asks the tough questions of organisations on how they are designing and using their technology. Guiding digital journeys in adapting to humanising IT, Simone blends business and technology approaches and frameworks to help us thrive in an ever-changing, dynamic world. Enabling humans to flourish and have exceptional experiences are her active values – ensuring people are connected, knowledge is shared, and possibilities are discovered and potential realised. Simone takes things beyond technology by combining it with her HR, learning and development (L&D), organisational change and complementary health background for a deep leadership experience.

  A recognised Top 25 Industry Thought Leader, Women in DevOps list, Women in Tech award nominee, Simone is the editorial director of "The Youth Rise in Power" and "The Era of Humanizing IT" documentaries, a contributing author to *VeriSM: Unwrapped and Applied*, and ITIL® 4 High-Velocity IT and other international certifications, DevOps Institute ebooks and a contributing reviewer for the European Commission and Cynefin-based field guide on "Managing complexity (and chaos) in times of crisis".

- **Matt Beran:**
  Matt Beran has over 20 years' experience in service management and customer service. He is known for challenging industry norms, practical advice and unique approaches to service management.

  Matt is the host of Ticket Volume, a weekly podcast about IT and is a highly regarded speaker. His favourite topics introduce new ways of thinking about service experiences and improving teamwork.

I would also like to thank Patrik Šolc, for his helpful feedback during the production of this book.

CONTENTS

CHAPTER 1: YOU'RE NOT ALONE

Thank you for purchasing *An Education in Service Management.*

My name is David Barrow, and I've been working in IT service-related roles for 30 years. Over that time, I've seen IT shift from being in the basement to being a critical enablement function embedded into every organisation and our way of life globally and beyond.

The change has been staggering, but as someone who's worked within the industry for a long time, I've seen ways of working, standards and legislation far outstripped by the evolution of IT.

How, why, where and when we use IT has come on in leaps and bounds. IT has blurred the lines between professional and personal, and our ability to interact, learn and be entertained can now all be achieved through a single device. Yet, in the workplace, our methods to deliver these as IT services have progressed slowly by comparison.

Technology is innovative, progressive, has no bias, and continually improves due to the innovation and evolution of human intelligence. However, how we work together and provide opportunity and inclusion is left behind due to dips in human intelligence as we sometimes revert to safety or tribalism.

I write this book in the context of 'IF'. I ask myself 'IF' someone will pick this up, 'IF' they will choose to read it and 'IF' they will find it helpful. I have no idea if anyone will do these things, and as an 'author', I'm sure I'm not alone in thinking that.

I've chosen to face this challenge as I realise that the challenges we have today, in or out of work, will have been met and conquered by others. If service management has taught me one thing, it's that we can learn more from looking at the past than we can by simply sitting and wondering about our future. I want to use that past to inform our future.

We make our future through a mixture of judgement based on experience and judgement based on our gut feeling and no small amount of luck.

We can improve our probability of success by sharing our thoughts, experiences, failures and successes, which is one of the purposes of this publication.

Therefore, I wanted to write this book from my perspective as an IT service professional of 30 years while also placing myself in the shoes of my intended readers (though I'm happy for anyone to pick this up).

Suppose you have picked up the book as an IT or service management professional, wondering how and why to progress your career into or within service management.

You're not alone in wondering:

- What is next in my career?
- Will I fail?
- Is that a stupid question?
- Is service management a boring job?
- Which industries can I work in?
- Can I work anywhere?
- Why do they do it this way?
- Which certifications should I take?
- How do I implement what I've learned?

- How can I share this?

My hope during our journey together is that you'll learn about all of this and more.

Alternatively, if you have picked the book up as an organisational or IT leader and are wondering how and why to progress with your digital transformation or service management integration or what to do next, then worry not.

You're not alone in wondering:

- What is IT service management (ITSM)?
- Why do people think service management is valuable?
- How will service management enable my organisation?
- How can service management inform my strategy?
- How can service management help solve organisational problems?
- How does service management help with customer issues?
- What sort of service management professional should I recruit?
- How can we use service management to share success?
- How can I empower my teams?
- What next for my teams and me?

IT is a business-critical function; we deliver experiences, stimulate strategic shifts, and protect people and organisations from theft, cyber attacks and the related regulatory, reputational and financial impacts. These are just the tip of the iceberg.

ITSM is a critical element of 'IT' that is often misunderstood. In this publication, I and my network of associates, contacts, partners and customers will seek to demystify ITSM and help you understand how:

- Working in or with ITSM can enable you to build a career that spans global industries, allowing you to work anywhere on anything; and
- Developing a career in ITSM can lead you from service desk analyst to chief technology officer, entrepreneur, author, YouTuber – you can go anywhere you want from any starting point.

How you, as a chief technology officer (CTO), chief information officer (CIO) or organisational leader, can enable your teams to deliver exceptional digital experiences that delight your consumers, your partners, and your present and future customers.

It's important to me to discuss these topics. More to help you as the reader understand the themes highlighted above and those below that are continually coming up, whether it be via my network of colleagues or customers or my network from The itSMF UK, the British Computer Society (BCS), the British Standards Institute (BSI) or the International Organization for Standardization (ISO).

I'll cover these questions and points plus more throughout this book, framed through my 30 years of experience and that of others.

We'll take a journey that covers elements such as the following:

- How I and others came to work within ITSM.
- How I failed exams and misapplied my ITSM certifications.

- How ITSM isn't just taking a course and passing an exam.
- Why leaders must empower their teams to innovate, govern, measure and pivot.
- How ITSM can make or break entire enterprise organisations,[2] prevent accidents and detect disasters.
- How service management can save the lives of humans and animals.
- How the power of community can be harnessed to co-create organisational value.

This book aims to demystify ITSM as an organisational enabler. I also aim to help those breaking into service management or those already on a service management career path by showing its challenges and how exciting it can be. Further, we will discuss how vital service management is as an industry to enterprise leaders in enabling digital transformation and innovation.

I look forward to hearing your feedback on the book and working with you in the future as part of a global service management Community of Practice (CoP).

---

[2] An enterprise organisation is a large business that has the size and resources to dominate a specific market and is characterised by being high revenue and having many employees.

CHAPTER 2: WHAT IS ITSM?

What is ITSM? It's a great question that I have been asked throughout my career. Here are four scenarios where I've been asked the question and struggled to find an answer:

- ***"So, what do you do for a living?"***
  Friends or acquaintances often ask me. In some cases, they've asked me this for years. Some genuinely think I work in some clandestine intelligence role, as I used to work in the public sector; others just get lost as I try to explain how I turn IT into a service.
- ***"I'm not sure what he does for a living; he's on the phone often and once spent a weekend calling some divers out to get rid of some sharks."***
  My wife, when attempting to explain what I do to the friends mentioned above and acquaintances and family members. Who then asked me "How's work?" and little else as they didn't want to get into it.
- ***"What is service management as a career? How much will I earn, and where could I end up?"***
  As asked by apprentices, graduates and professionals looking to understand their options when making career moves.
- ***"What will service management do that will enhance my organisation and delight my customers?"***
  This question was asked of me at senior management

and C-level when I proposed enterprise service management as a way of working.

In this book, I plan to tackle these questions and so much more; we'll have varying levels of detail, some examples of my own and the opinions of others, plus a few infographics.

Coming from these angles will help us build a rounded view of service management, its benefits to all, and its future. Together we'll become educated in service management.

The history of service management

I'll begin by taking a brief look at human history regarding professions. It is correct to point out that I'm no historical expert. Still, I expect you'll join me in recognising that as I write this in 2023, IT has been around for approximately 100 years. IT is a young industry and as such as has several even younger career paths.

Let's begin with a quick understanding of the evolution of humans and our professions.

A quick search via a popular search engine informs us of the following:

- Toolmaking is considered one of the world's oldest professions at approximately 2.8 million years. Early civilisations needed to hunt and build a shelter – and hands alone were not up to the job. [3]
- Tailors and seamstresses were recognised as a profession approximately 500,000 years ago. Looking

---

[3] *https://www.newscientist.com/article/mg22530064-500-human-ancestors-got-a-grip-on-tools-3-million-years-ago/*.

good is the key to feeling good, something the ancient Egyptians cottoned on to early (pun intended).[4]

- Ceramicists were recognised as a profession approximately 26,000 years ago. They were cooking, eating and drinking from solid vessels, which made you less likely to spill something on your finely tailored clothing.[5]

You may argue that IT was around before the mid-1900s, but I expect you'd agree that it only existed as a profession per se in the 1940s as part of Allied war efforts during the 2nd World War. These were the first times people were working on operating technology that delivered information quickly into the hands of humans.

As the delivery of IT became ordinary in the latter half of the 20th century, so did several job roles within the industry. Most of these roles were based upon the operation of IT on aspects such as mainframe operation and maintenance; this later evolved into the development and commercialisation of software.

As governments and organisations began to utilise IT to run their organisations, the concept of 'services' began to evolve, and ITSM was 'born' with the likes of the IT Infrastructure Library (ITIL) as a methodology being an answer to several pressing questions around the delivery of IT as a service.

Since then, IT has become a tool that has weaved its way into our everyday lives; we interact with IT all day, every day.

---

[4] *https://www.oldest.org/people/professions/*.

[5] *https://link.springer.com/referenceworkentry/10.1007/978-3-030-44600-0_32-1*.

It's in our homes that were built with tools; we catalogue, order and deliver clothing using IT. Those vessels that were first made approximately 26,000 years ago are fired using electronic kiln controllers, or in some cases, we circumvent the need for clay through 3D printing.

Incredibly, this 'thing' called IT has weaved into our everyday lives, and yet it has only existed for 100 years, and we've squeezed so much out of it, but there is so much more to come.

As I'm a big fan of a picture, I enclose a 'not to scale' timeline that I hope illustrates the relative 'age' of our industry and service management as a profession.

For over 2.8 million years, toolmaking will have evolved to the point where we all understand its value, core accountabilities and possible career path; the same applies to tailoring/seamstress work and ceramics.

By comparison, not only is IT as a profession a relative infant but service management as a profession is half its age again. It's no wonder we have much growing up to do, and relatively little is known about our profession.

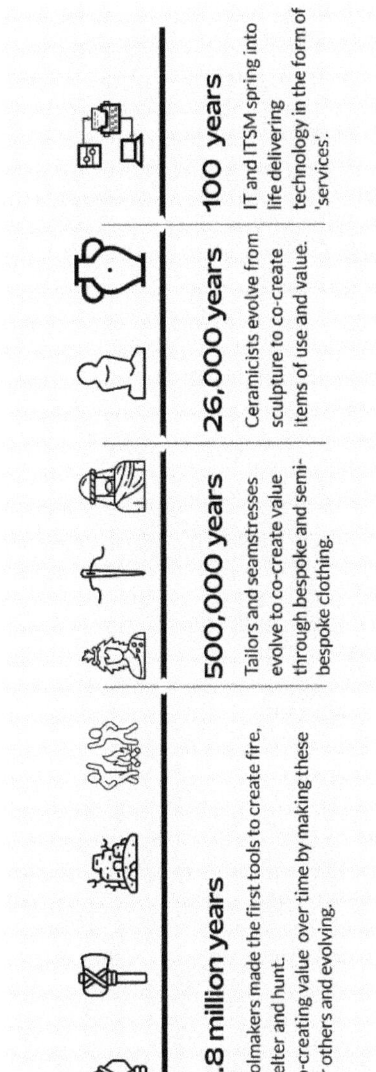

Figure 1: A Comparison of Professions

As I write in 2023, ITSM has been used for approximately 40 years. It looks at strategising, designing and operating services for your customers; it's about handling the risk for your customers, managing the design of IT services, and co-creating value to enable desired customer outcomes. Additionally, ITSM has elements of controlled experimentation that are necessary to improve and evolve continually.

That's a lot to take in, but it is ITSM summed up for me.

IT has evolved so rapidly that terms such as 'the information age' or 'the fourth industrial revolution' are often used. Along with this, our approaches to work are rapidly transforming.

Take, for example, all the changes within the last few decades. It was way back in 1989 that the first version of the ITIL emerged. It was partly in response to the UK government's desire to standardise how we deliver IT 'services' and became the de-facto approach to what became known as IT service management or ITSM.

ITIL v2 followed in 2001, ITIL v3 in 2007, and ITIL v4 in 2019.

As ITSM evolved, so did the ways of delivering IT services. 'Lean' processes emerged in 1991, with the Agile Manifesto launched by a group of software engineers in 2001.

Service integration and management (SIAM) was developed in 2005. An evolution was required as organisations entrusted multiple partners to deliver IT services; they needed a strategic approach to managing these suppliers via a single 'service integrator'.

Development operations (DevOps) was developed in 2007–2008 to improve an organisation's way of working when it came to delivering IT applications and services in a speedy and controlled manner.

And so, as we arrive into 2023, we have witnessed an evolution occurring over approximately 40 years, which in some cases has led to us reverting to our ancestral behaviours of forming tribes.

Are you ITIL, lean, DevOps, or the recently released VeriSM (value-driven, evolving, responsive, integrated service management)?

We will discuss these methodologies and behaviours further as we progress.

What is a service?

I've worked in and around IT for 30 years, and while I consider myself a technologist, I also consider myself a 'service' person. It drives me; helping someone defines a service. I get out of bed to delight my customers.

From my days working on helpdesks, where I was helping a new customer every two minutes, until today as a consultant, my service approach has evolved but has yet to change fundamentally. Everyone has a slightly different definition of service, usually based on your belief system as much as the 'service' you seek to procure or use.

In my case, I want to delight people; I also want to be delighted.

There are purely transactional services, such as buying a train ticket, that both humans and IT facilitate. Purchasing a ticket for a journey is a service where the key to success is often expediency; you are travelling and want a ticket to your destination, and you may need it within one minute as the train arrives.

Alternatively, you may need assistance with your journey, you may be stressed, running late and in need of urgent help – you require a different level of service, and how that's delivered to you matters; your requirement from this service evolves from a purely transactional service to a much more interactive service that requires some appropriate responses to your predicament.

Through this one service 'type', we have seen how a service requirement can diversify to become more than one type of service dependent upon the scenario.

Is IT a service?

Over the years, we have sought to automate such services as travel and ticketing through IT. Purchasing a ticket is an appropriate scenario that defines IT as a service. A great deal goes on via IT behind the scenes, though we only see a ticket to our destination in the end.

Removing the human element can reduce wait times, increase expediency and allow the human part to be more readily available to service those in need.

It's for scenarios like this that service management is so valuable.

Let's consider the facilitation of train travel as an IT service; what goes into that? I want to start by covering how the service management function can influence the lifecycle of an IT service at a high level:

- **Service strategy** – In this case, the train company wants to take a strategic approach to facilitate travel and ticketing transactions. Service management can be used to align IT to this strategy and provide an early voice in support or, indeed, to propose an alternate strategic approach that could use or reuse an existing IT service.

- **Service design** – Service management uses its knowledge of operating IT services daily to inform the design of the new digital service. It works closely with development teams to create a service that meets the organisation's desired strategic and operational outcomes. They capture and co-create requirements and expected service levels by mapping the customer journey.
- **Service transition** – Service management assists in transitioning the service, working on its testing with developers and pilot customers, preparing the digital service for release and working on advance communications and training materials for those supporting the service and those consuming it.
- **Service operation** – Service management is part of a team supporting the service when it's rolled out to customers. Supporting the service may be answering customers' calls, working with suppliers and vendors, and providing feedback to the board from customers of the service.
- **Continual improvement** – Service management will capture customer feedback and experiences and seek to improve the digital service. It will work across operational teams, and with suppliers, vendors and customer groups to both continually improve the service

and manage it through improvement into retirement – yes, IT services can be retired just like us humans.

- **Knowledge management** – Service management is forever capturing knowledge, using it to help service consumers who have issues, or using it to develop service propositions through continual improvement and also using it to cycle back into service strategy and service design when redeveloping existing services or designing and creating even more digital services.

Simply put, a well-run service management function is involved in every aspect of an IT service's lifecycle.

These aspects, as well as those of IT service development, innovation and the more recent scenarios of handheld consumer-driven digital IT services, suggest to me that IT is just as much a service as any other industry, and service management is a critical factor in enabling an excellent service experience.

The difference between service management and project management

Throughout my career, I have worked on projects and significant work programmes. Project management and ITSM should spend a lot of time working together.

Project management is primarily concerned with taking something from its beginning to its end via a series of controlled and time-managed tasks that ultimately result in an acceptable endpoint. Project management is mainly time bound in terms of delivery and qualitative in terms of delivering a series of requirements by the end of the period.

Service management often works with and within project management. Some of service management's primary goals in this context are to:

- Ensure any new project delivering IT digital services meets the requirements of its consumers;
- Ensure any new project delivering IT digital services meets the organisational strategic intentions and goals;
- Ensure any new project delivering IT digital services is operational, governable and respects any required regulatory standards; and
- Ensure any new project delivering IT digital services is handed over appropriately to operational teams so they can pick it up on Day 1 and improve it throughout its service lifecycle.

Although not exhaustive, the elements above illustrate how important it is that project management and service management collaborate to co-create value with the IT digital service recipients. Only by doing this can they co-create value in the provision, operation and ongoing improvement of IT services to their consumers and customers.

The author's entry into service management

Now is an excellent point to discuss my entry into service management approximately 23 years ago, in 2000.

My first seven years in the workplace were a real mix of IT roles. My career began when I secured my first full-time job in 1993 as a 16-year-old who left school with few qualifications. I attended a practice interview as part of a school leavers' job scheme, and I was asked the question,

"Can you build a PC?" My response was, "Yes." Though I didn't expect the following statement to be – "Go and build one in that room!"

In truth, I did have an affinity for technology as a youngster. I'd figured out how to make all of the school computers in my class play Axel F (from a CD in a magazine I'd bought) and I had done some related work experience. I'd dabbled in the rubber keyboards of a Spectrum PC.

On that day, I built quite a few PCs. I'd seen some MS-DOS and Windows 3.11 installation discs and I also set about installing these on every PC. I had quite the production line going when I saw a head pop around the door an hour later. They'd expected that I'd been struggling when I'd been having a great time. My only error was not wearing anything for anti-static, though nothing wrong ever came of it.

With that, I was offered my first full-time job and started weeks before receiving my GCSE results (luckily). My starting salary was **£40 per week**, which was approximately £9 less than my numerous newspaper and magazine delivery rounds. I kept both jobs for as long as I could.

I was over the moon.

I will only bore you with some details of my next steps. I outgrew that role in a two-person business and moved on to coding for a slightly larger company that supplied sales, vehicle service and maintenance software to the motor trade.

As coders go, I was useless, but those six months of attempting to code would stay with me and serve me well. The relationships I'd built with our customers led to my installing computer systems into our customers' garages.

For me, this was great: I got a company vehicle (one I could squeeze my motorbike into), and I got paid to drive around the country, drilling holes in walls and feeding cables into computer systems. I'd disturb the peace at night by exploring the area on my motorbike.

It was a great time that was sadly curtailed when I was a passenger in a car accident and couldn't drive for a while. As a result of my lack of mobility, I was 'temporarily' moved to the helpdesk.

At first, the thought of being tied to a phone in the office was awful. However, those times on-site gave me quite the advantage. Customers who called the helpdesk knew my face, and I knew their systems (and all of the errors I'd made when on-site). Working on the helpdesk was great. It developed my service mindset and led to me becoming an information technology trainer.

Becoming a trainer continued me on the service path. At around this time, the home PC was becoming more common. Part of my job was training the general public, giving me a unique insight into how much IT was unknown at the time. It also made me more comfortable when in face-to-face meetings and more adaptable when asked leftfield questions.

To fast forward, this role led to my working for IBM Global Services, where I received an education in business and IT services. IBM does things the right way.

My break into service management came when I was asked to contribute to some processes for IBM's largest helpdesk at that time. It was at this point that my prior experience came together. I understood development, service transition and knowledge, and how to handle people – and I built this into my processes. When those processes were signed off, I became an IBM service management professional; it's still one of my proudest achievements.

Summary

I hope that by learning a little about the history of ITSM, its origins as a service, its interactions with other disciplines and my journey, you'll have started to form your idea on what makes a good service manager and what makes service management so valuable as an enabler of IT services to consumers, customers and colleagues.

Later in the book, we'll dive into more detail about what makes a great service management professional from several perspectives. We'll also cover common service management elements, how ITSM can enable organisations, and much more. I hope it provides insight into those suitable for the role(s) and why service management is so valuable to today's organisations.

CHAPTER 3: COMMON SERVICE MANAGEMENT ELEMENTS

As we progress through this book, I'll attempt to use the words 'Information Technology Service Management' (ITSM) together at the appropriate time and in the relevant context. This will be a conscious decision on my part. Let me explain why.

ITSM is the common acronym used to describe service management. When IT became commonplace in organisations in the 1980s into the 2000s, the term 'IT' was undoubtedly the most appropriate descriptor of our work. IT was predominately a tool that was used to 'do' business.

What I mean by this is that IT was more likely to have been used to deliver business functions such as the following:

- Payroll.
- Finance/end-of-month reconciliation.
- Transacting on a deal or trade.
- Tracking goods.
- Point of sale.
- Booking an appointment.

This list is not exhaustive, but it was commonplace for these more transactional functions to be delivered via IT at the 'back-end' of an organisation.

Incident and knowledge management

I remember a time when I could work in IT without a computer. I once worked on a helpdesk with just a pen and a piece of paper using a pre-prepared 'docket' as a document to log my ticket, which I would then physically pass to my colleagues when I couldn't solve the query. In service management terms, this 'problem' would be called an 'incident'. I expect you'll know this already.

This was an incredibly efficient system as my colleagues would note down the solution and file it as appropriate for later use, or they would capture the planned date/time to visit the customer and return it to me for their file.

We had a critical service management element in place, namely knowledge management, before I'd even heard of it. At this time, and in this case, IT was not used as the enabler of the organisation. However, our core service skills and IT knowledge and experience enabled the organisation to support and deliver its IT services to its customers.

As the industry has evolved, this scenario is incredibly different today.

How we use IT now enables our people to gather, document and access knowledge that serves our enterprise, its customers and consumers at such a pace that it is unrecognisable from my scenario of 25 years ago.

Maybe it's better if I explain via an infographic:

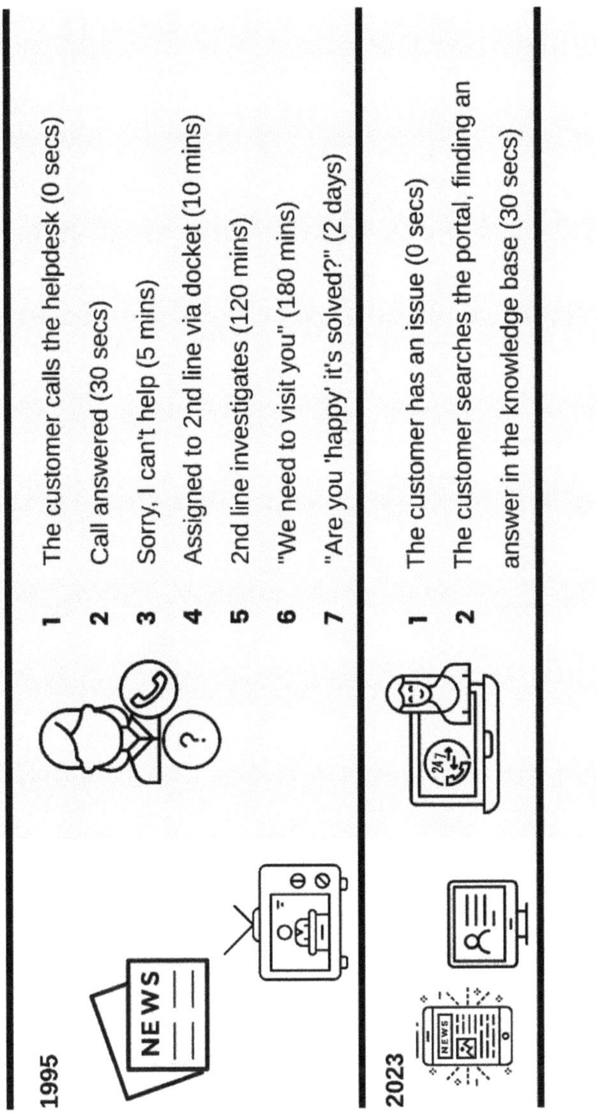

Figure 2: A Helpdesk Call Comparison of 1995 to 2023

This simple scenario covers a similar event seemingly 28 years apart. In truth, this still happens today, even if it's now less manual in its approach.

In my earlier example, I discussed how effective our paper process was all those years ago; its only downside was its most critical success factor, the 'experience' for the customer.

Customers of IT services were usually expectant of this poor level of service, which is why our industry was not seen as enabling the organisation or its customers. Here, we have a customer calling the helpdesk. Unfortunately, I cannot help; their query joins the list of questions in the queue for second line support.

Our method was as follows: I leave my desk (therefore delaying an answer to my next call) and go to another room. While there, I grab five minutes chatting about the weekend's events, pass my docket onto their 'to-do list' and go back to my phone.

The second line works through their list, calling customers back and informing those they cannot help on the telephone that they need to visit the customer. This visit could be a six-hour drive each way, depending on the location of the customer, and only take 15 minutes to resolve.

Not only was this a long wait for the customer, but it could also have been more efficient for them and my organisation, who covered the cost of time, fuel, hotels, meals, etc. This is partly why my employer ended up selling support packages that cost as much as the IT systems themselves (an early form of service management).

'Modern' incident and knowledge management as a service

Let's fast forward to 2023.

That same customer can now summarise their issue in an online portal available 24/7/365. The portal contains all similar incidents and provides several responses that the customer can attempt. More often than not, they can resolve their issue using this service. Where they cannot do so, our chatbot can engage an agent to help, who can remotely take over the customer's machine and deliver a solution in moments.

In 2023, the engagement shortens; in both 1995 and 2023, a customer and an agent exist with the means to help one another via several mediums to suit the customer at a time to serve them. The customer is most likely to still be unhappy at the initial issue, but they are much more likely to have had a positive experience than their 1995 self.

In this case, service management has been used to deliver an improved service level experience, using concepts such as knowledge management and continual improvement to provide a solution immediately using continually improved iterations of process and technology from 1995 to today.

Service management has saved time and cost for the customer and the organisation. In this scenario, service management has enabled the organisation. This is a form of 'enterprise'- focused service management – less focused purely on IT and more focused on a 'service' that enables the customer to remain productive as much as possible.

I've chosen this scenario as it's fairly simplistic but it shows the actual 'value' of service management. Key to my explanation is the service management practice of 'continual improvement'.

Service management as a practice has continually improved over the years, taking the various iterations of methodologies such as ITIL, VeriSM, Agile, etc., not to mention that those performing service management roles have improved by using the continual improvement ethos, not least myself.

I'd now like to cover a few key service management practice areas, and I'd like to discuss where I have got it wrong before I've begun to get it right.

Service management governance as a service

Where to begin? I plan to start with governance, as it's a considerable element of any service management professional's role. Governance is how an organisation is directed and controlled.

Governance is a big part of the role of a service management professional as it defines the expected directions, policies and rules the organisation uses to deliver and maintain its digital IT services.

It is an element of service management I have chosen to call out as I have misapplied it several times. Before I discuss this, let's cover what 'governance' seemingly means in the parlance of service management.

Service management governance is widely recognised as a means of achieving regulatory or organisational governance requirements through managing internal and external stakeholders and services throughout an organisation. Service management governance engages stakeholders and delivery channels for effectively managing risks or issues.

Even though service management has historically focused on IT services, this approach can apply to accounting, business administration and other service areas. Undertaking governance enables the monitoring and control of risk, value and cost, whether the cost is regulatory or reputational.

In my case, I have misapplied governance, turning it into a line that cannot be crossed under any circumstance. Doing so has meant that I have stifled innovation and experimentation where I have felt that a new or amended IT service is, in my mind, too 'risky' to deploy.

When I did this, I had the right intentions. I've worked in industries where a wrong move could cost my organisations billions of pounds or result in the digital service I manage ending up on the front page of the tabloid newspapers. Working in service management can sometimes come with a burden of responsibility that turns a usually laid-back character into an incredibly risk-averse stakeholder, and this was me.

As service management knowledge and practices have evolved around me, I've switched this risk-averseness to be more focused on risk awareness, using this as an opportunity to seek out the potential for opportunity and innovation.

Please do not mistake this for callousness.

It's the benefit of experience and trust in the incredibly talented people around me that allows me to use service management as a driver to deliver the intended organisational value, working with corporate leaders, vendors and their expert teams to provide decisions that are made and enforced in a dynamic business environment.

Elsewhere in this book, we discuss the IT digital service lifecycle. It is here where service management can make a real difference.

In many cases, service management governance is most widely first applied as an element of 'service transition'.

Service transition is the act of service management assisting in transitioning the service, working on its testing with developers and pilot customers, preparing the digital service for release and working on advance communications and training materials for those supporting the service and those consuming the service.

If this is the first time service management becomes involved, it may also be the first time any form of 'governance' is applied. Therefore, I've learned that we should shift the value of service management to 'the left', moving it as early as possible into the IT digital service lifecycle. I'd suggest taking it into 'service strategy'.

When service management is working with sales, marketing, development and the board on developing this strategy, we can come together to build a joined-up view of risk and governance and bake these elements into the design of the IT service.

Through doing this, we are all on the same page and reduce the risk to the service and the organisation as we progress through service transition and into service operation. We reduce the chances of any last-minute risks being escalated and better prepare ourselves to deliver, operate and continually improve an IT service that enables the organisation, its employees and service consumers.

Service management and IT change

If I've misapplied service management governance, I have seriously misapplied service management and IT change or 'change management', as it was better known.

In essence, change management or 'change enablement', as it is now better known, is the act of reviewing, scheduling and approving a change to existing IT services or the rollout and go-live of new IT services – not to mention the retirement and maintenance of IT services.

I've fulfilled the IT change manager role on a few occasions, and I've been in and around change management for 25 years. For some of that period, I have been an obstacle to change for the same reasons I misapplied service management governance. I was risk averse but added to that, I was also lacking the confidence to hold my hand up and say, "I don't understand what you are doing."

Change management involves many people within its process, who could be people such as:

- Change requester.
- Change implementor.
- Change tester.
- Customer impacted by the change.
- Vendors.
- Service managers.
- Problem managers.
- Incident managers.
- Change manager.

The list above is not exhaustive as it depends on your organisation and your change type, but I hope it demonstrates that several people are involved in a single change – and there is often more than one change happening at any time.

The majority of change reviews and approvals/dismissals happen at the change advisory board (CAB) or change approval board (CAB) meetings and would be chaired by a change manager with all of the parties above present.

As a change manager, I ran a tight ship; nothing got through my CAB approval without my reviewing it in depth. This tight ship made sure every change was thoroughly inspected before approval, and if I'm honest, it would often be an awful meeting to attend for those trying to advance their request for change (RFC).

Looking back, I feel embarrassed as my lack of confidence meant I rarely, if ever, said,

"I don't understand what you are doing – please, can you help me understand it?"

My approach was to let something come to CAB meetings and to find every reason to deny the change if I couldn't piece it together myself. Part of me was doing this for the right reasons, wanting to protect my organisation or client, but another part was a lack of knowledge and stubbornness to admit this.

As I grew confident, I began to look at change requests as early as possible, seeking to understand the risk of doing the change as well as the risk of **not** doing the change. My approach changed to aiming to understand more through capturing knowledge via conversation with change requestors and those customers potentially impacted. In doing this, I was able to increase the velocity of change, vastly improve the CAB process and still be risk-appropriate in my approach.

Over the years, both I and change management have evolved. Change management has been suitably rebadged to change enablement, and this rebrand is beginning to pay dividends. As a service management consultant, I've seen others adopt my earlier approach. Using my own experiences, I've understood why and intervened appropriately, providing feedback on how I used to do things the wrong way and how I used service management principles to improve the practice and myself.

In one scenario, we brought a seemingly siloed set of functions together to increase the velocity of change and deliver real value to an organisation – this from a process often disregarded or derided as adding zero value to the organisation.

In another organisation, we took a team placed on the change management 'watchlist' for almost a year due to their perceived 'fail fast' nature and turned them into a 'fail fast, fail safe' team within eight weeks. We did this by looking at the client's digital services and way of working at a holistic level; doing so enabled us to build an understanding of its people, knowledge, consumer needs and third-party partners. We were then able to bridge the relationship gap with the process owners. By doing this, we effectively removed silos preventing teams from working together by agreeing on shared change management objectives and language. Ultimately, this team became the flag bearers for the methods to deliver innovation and continual development throughout the organisation's change enablement process.

Much of this was achieved through effective communication and implementing lessons learned from our years of experience. I hope this will become more apparent and have added relevance to you as we discuss further service management elements and ways of working throughout this book.

Service management and the watermelon effect

Those of you reading this who have worked in or around service management may well be aware of the 'watermelon effect' concerning management information and reporting; please humour me while I cover it from my perspective.

For years, I have presented what is most commonly known as 'service reviews' to customers and colleagues alike. In these IT service reviews, we will typically cover several areas of the service. Often, I have taken over these reviews from others. More recently, I have worked with customers and colleagues to define and redefine those areas that merit a service review. While doing this, I've seen the error of my ways in the past.

A service review is usually a monthly event that captures actions and updates from that month, and closes old actions and provides updates on aspects such as:

- IT Service(s) – availability for the period.
- IT Service(s) – unplanned outages during the period.
- Mean time to respond (MTTR) to IT Service(s) outages during the period.
- Mean time to resolve (confusingly also MTTR) to IT service(s) outages during the period.
- Customer satisfaction related to the IT Service(s) during the period.
- Changes to the IT Service(s) during the period.
- Continual improvements activities relating to the IT service(s) during the period.

- A forward view of the above as part of an IT Service(s) roadmap.

Once again, this list is not exhaustive, merely indicative of the types of things discussed at this monthly event. The event usually involves much effort associated with compiling the data, which is generally presented by a service manager/service delivery manager.

This role is one of the 'givens' in the job and can be a nerve-wracking experience, though its less nerve-wracking when you are presenting a bunch of 'green' measures, for example:

Table 1: Example Service Availability

Service Name	Reporting Period	Service Availability Target	Service Availability Measure
A Service	01/23	99.7%	99.8%
A Service	02/23	99.7%	99.7%

Here, 'A Service' has met its service availability target for two months in a row. Hurrah, this one will be an easy conversation. Imagine the dismay of the presenter when an audible 'tut' and a shake of the head are offered in response. Something that has happened to me on more than one occasion. It's frankly soul-destroying for all involved.

On the one hand, you are delivering to your targets; these are in the contract, widely known and what you are paid to do. On the other hand, that 99.8% availability during the period 01/23 was a nearly 90-minute outage during a critical monthly event.

As for the 99.7% availability reported during 02/23, this 'green' measure comes with an outage period of 130 minutes that not only came during a critical business event but was also caused by a failed change that, although unknown to the organisation, had been approved by the IT team within the impacted organisation.

Yes, in both cases, this is the reality of the situation. Those I was reporting to didn't necessarily know about the failed change (neither did I!) but their teams and customers had reported that the service was failing and felt the pain for a cumulative total of 220 minutes (3 hours 40 minutes) across two monthly reporting cycles.

This is a 'watermelon service level agreement'(SLA) – that is, it is green on the outside, but from the customers' all-so-important perspective, it's red on the inside as the IT service regularly disables them instead of enabling them and their productivity.

While I'm using a fairly straightforward example here, it is common. Simply put, SLAs are often part of a package. Whether that's a package supplied by an IT services provider or part of an IT service design package created as a service takes shape. In both cases, they are a point-in-time measurement.

To move away from service management and the watermelon effect, we must build a clearer understanding of our services – and deliver them as a service with the appropriate measures as befits their value-focused service outcomes. This is where delivering IT as a service becomes more 'real world'.

We must design services aligned with those value-focused outcomes, much like we experience services in the real world. If you go out for fast food, you are more likely to value the availability of the product and the speed you receive it than its fine-dining experience – in essence, both products are similar. Still, they are wrapped in a different service offering, a 'service wrap'.

In our everyday lives, we make value-focused choices based on real-time information and desires; the volume of information and our desires often change, as do our service choices – we certainly don't wait for around approximately 45 days (as we often do in IT) to look back at events.

By learning from the real world, we can adopt and adapt our IT service management measures and construct/reconstruct measures that are appropriate to the services we deliver. We can also use this information to drive value-focused conversations which co-create value on a real-time basis as opposed to looking backwards every 45 days or so.

This activity once again begins in the IT service lifecycle stage – service strategy. It may be that the organisation is willing to accept this level of service; if they are and it's documented, you can refer your customer to this and work together to amend the mindset.

However, suppose you can make a case for real-time, value-focused adaptable reporting with associated IT services. In that case, you can deliver a more innovative approach that removes the watermelon effect and delights your customers – it also saves a lot of manual labour every month.

You may be reading this and thinking, "Sounds good, but how do I do that?" I hope to shed light on this in the next section.

Service management reporting – and influencing

As you'll see in this book, management information and reporting are among service management's givens. How, when and why we present information is vital from a few perspectives. Most commonly, these are:

- Day-to-day service operations – Is the service available, running to the desired speed, is disk space OK, and is any maintenance needed?
- Pro-active service operation – Do we have we a certificate to renew, a patch to install and a maintenance window to attend to?
- Pro-active service enhancements – New version release, service overhaul, etc.

You'll have grown used to my saying this; the above is not exhaustive. Much like the methodologies of service management, people will read a book such as this and either take the list as the de-facto need or endlessly debate the content. I'm not telling you what to report, more what is usually reported.

I make this point as I'm about to discuss more reporting – and influencing, and I'll aim to make some obvious points based on my mistakes and those of others.

Take a look at the table and think about what you see:

Table 2: Example Security Incidents

Service Name	Reporting Period	Security Incidents Reported	Increase/Decrease
Security Service A	01/23	450	N/A
Security Service A	02/23	600	33.33%
Security Service A	03/23	850	88.89%

This table is based on a real-world scenario. In this case, an organisation had invested in a new IT security service that a trusted partner ran; the table formed part of the first service reviews and was delivered every month, mid-month. Pulling together the information was fairly easy; presenting it was down to a senior member of the trusted partner's team. There were many other elements to the report, including service costs, and highlights, lowlights, but this table stuck out to me, and it turned out it stuck out to those that had invested in the service.

Service management is as much about reading between the lines as it is about reading the lines themselves. In this case, my role was merely that of an observer as I sought to understand the partnership, its aims and the outcomes that were required.

'Outcomes' is the appropriate word here; often, services are designed based on obvious elements; in this case, the obvious element was that an investment in a security service should result in a drop in security incidents being reported. Before I go on, let us define an 'incident' in the context of ITSM.

Incident: an incident is an unplanned interruption to a service or reduction in the quality of service.

The above is widely accepted as the definition of an incident in the world of ITSM.

As this service was bedded in, there had been an element of understanding that the detection of security incidents would increase by a third; surely, we were becoming more aware of incidents impacting the organisation? The minutes of a previous meeting had suggested this figure would drop once we had arrived into month three.

As you can see, the figure didn't drop. In this scenario, the influence of this reporting was leading to questions regarding the validity of the investment in this security service. Surely such an investment should bear fruit by month three and certainly not see a huge increase in reported incidents. Questions were asked as to whether the investment should be withdrawn.

As an observer and somebody new to the organisation, I was able to ask a question from the point of ignorance (though, in this case, it was educated based on my own past mistakes).

My question was simple:

"Is this table telling us what we think it is – that the number of security incidents reported has risen almost 89% in 3 months?"

This question was met with a good response from the trusted partner:

"Could we take this offline and come back to you later today?"

This response was good for this scenario as it did not commit the presenter to an immediate answer but placed a time on the response, which the audience was now keen to find out.

We worked together and two hours later had our answer, and with a little more collaboration, our table looked like this by the end of the day:

Table 3: Example Security Events Detected

Service Name	Reporting Period	Security Events Detected & Remediated Without Impact	Increase/ Decrease
Security Service A	01/23	450	N/A

Security Service A	02/23	600	33.33% ⇧
Security Service A	03/23	850	88.89% ⇧

Hopefully, the difference is immediately obvious. What had actually been happening was a great news story; this new service had been proactively detecting and remediating security incidents with no impact on the organisation – and it had increased this by almost 89% in 3 months.

We cross-referenced this information with the service desk team, and we were able to quickly establish that the number of security-related incidents reported to the service desk had dropped considerably.

What had been seen to be a potential disaster was a great success.

Ultimately, this mix-up came down to the report's title and the column titles; it was designed to be a report on events, not incidents. Another contributory factor was the report itself, and those gathering the information, had not considered the impact or benefit to the enterprise as a whole; by reaching out to the service desk and asking for input, we could see a real good-news story for the organisation, its consumers and its partner.

Event management is a key proactive way of monitoring and detecting potential incidents on IT services – often, its success is measured by what it prevents and how that enables the organisation, as was the case here.

In this case, the organisation's enablement was that fewer security events were resulting in an impact on those consuming the service, reducing its risk of data loss and improving its ability to serve consumers.

In addition, we were also able to point out that all of this information was available in a 'real-time' view via a dashboard. This moved the monthly meeting from a look back over 45 days of history to a look at today's events with any exceptions discussed – of which there were few.

From a service management perspective, the technical design of this service became a case of referral for future successful event management implementations; however, its reporting and management information version 1.0 became a case of what not to do.

Summary

My aim within this chapter has been to provide a working understanding of ITSM and those elements of it that are most commonly used within organisations. I've chosen not to dive into the details of practices or processes, as you can find guides to these in other publications focusing on achieving service management certification.

We have seen how things have drastically changed over the last two to three decades and how it can be easy to misapply elements of service management in a manner that detracts from organisational value as opposed to enabling it.

My experience proves that just because you get something wrong shouldn't mean you cannot put it right. It's our duty as service management professionals to take ownership and correct our mistakes and those of others in a proactive manner akin to continual improvement.

Enterprise and organisational leadership enable this action by empowering their team members to undertake controlled experimentation and learn from it, as long as this aligns with the organisational strategy and risk appetite.

Ultimately, we should communicate appropriately, working with colleagues, customers, partners and consumers to view our services from the outside to the inside so that we can co-create value. Where we get it wrong, we should learn, move on and apply what we've learned.

This is continual improvement in action, and it's just one thing that makes service management so valuable.

CHAPTER 4: WHAT MAKES SERVICE MANAGEMENT SO VALUABLE?

As part of this book, we have and will continue to discuss many aspects of Service Management. I sincerely hope you'll already see why service management is valuable to organisations. I also hope you'll have noticed that service management is not merely an IT function but one that can be used to deliver results across the enterprise.

Service management is a relatively new profession that can take you into any organisation. Over the past decade, it been re-evaluated. Service management has grown, developed and is no longer part of the IT organisation exclusively; IT and digital services have become the organisation.

For those with ambition, working with an enterprise focus on service management can take you into any industry or company on the planet; from the boardroom at a bank, in government, or at your favourite sports team, you could be working anywhere and using service management as a platform to be a success.

In the hope that it will offer you a more rounded answer to the question of what makes service management so valuable, I have invited a number of my trusted connections to provide their thoughts from several perspectives. From here, I will independently add my view and round up the ideas of my connections.

From a Service Management Manager's Perspective

Doug Oram
IT Service Management Leader

"ITSM is valuable because it enables organisations to manage their IT services in a structured and efficient manner, ensuring that they meet the needs of the business (and its customers).

There is a multitude of reasons ITSM is extremely valuable, such as:

- *Alignment of IT and business: ITSM enables organisations to align their IT services with their business objectives, ensuring that IT can always support the organisation's goals and strategies.*
- *Increased efficiency and productivity: By standardising processes and procedures, ITSM can help organisations reduce duplication of effort, streamline workflows, and even automate tasks, leading to increased levels of efficiency and productivity.*
- *Service quality and customer satisfaction: ITSM processes are designed to improve service quality and customer satisfaction by ensuring that services are delivered consistently and to agreed levels, including the measurement of SLAs, KPIs and customer satisfaction ratings on an ongoing basis.*
- *Risk reduction: ITSM includes processes for identifying, assessing and managing risk, thus helping organisations to proactively mitigate potential issues and minimise the impact of incidents and changes, also ensuring that*

problem management and root cause analysis are being performed to reduce repeat issues/impacts.

- *Continuous service improvement: Last (but certainly not least) ITSM encourages organisations to constantly review and improve their IT services and related processes, enabling them to meet the changing needs of the business.*

Since ITSM provides a vast framework for managing IT services that is flexible, scalable and adaptable to the needs of each organisation, this is merely a handful of reasons it is extremely valuable. With the adoption of ITSM best practices, organisations can streamline and adapt their IT services to better support their business goals and deliver value to their customers."

From a Service Management Educator's Perspective

Suzanne D. Van Hove, Ed.D.
CEO/Founder, SED-IT

"Service management links the provider with the consumer in a manner that is beneficial to both parties. Evolving beyond "IT and the business", which still presumes two different organisations, the idea of 'service' is now at the forefront. Service management isn't about a specific framework, standard or methodology but rather it must continue to rise above the particulars to a <u>mindset</u> of service. That mindset is really asking the question, "How can I help?" and then making it happen.

Service management must focus on fulfilling needs efficiently and economically while ensuring the value proposition is achieved. Technology still plays a huge role (e.g., How do we exploit the capabilities of the continually disruptive and emerging technologies?), but the focus must be on the outcomes (and not the output) – it's about what can be achieved, not how it is achieved. I think that is the most important statement. What makes good service management useful is the focus on outcomes – what is needed and then achieved efficiently and economically."

From a Service Management Educator's Perspective

Suzanne Galletly
Portfolio Director at EXIN

"To answer this question, we need to consider the purpose of service management. Most people reading this book will probably have an ITSM background and will be familiar with the traditional view of ITSM as a set of processes to manage the design, planning and delivery of services. However, if we look at the higher purpose of service management, it is, of course, not about processes but about providing quality services that add value to the customer.

We also need to consider the changed context. In Economy 4.0, where digital technologies are creating rapid societal and economic changes, there is increasing pressure on organisations to adapt. Services are expected to be provided on-demand, user experience is paramount, and consumers have increasing power. Almost all services are, at least in part, 'digital'. From this broader viewpoint, service management is not only a crucial discipline to manage the provision of high-quality services; but can also be seen as a key enabler of transformation, digital or otherwise."

From a Service Management Educator's Perspective

Simone Jo-Moore
Humanising IT Expert

"Service management is always contextual. Hence why we often see 'IT' or 'product' in front of it in a field like technology. However, service management in and of itself is a profession that you'll find in any industry and organisation. It is a discipline in providing quality services and experiences for customers who value, buy and use them.

Now that's a very dry response to the 'what is' question. Let's take a more experiential view. The willingness not just to manage experiences, but go through them. If you enjoy building and managing the relationships, interactions with customers and the experience they have with the organisation you are in, then you'll find this profession extremely satisfying. It is about keeping the impact and influence on and by the human being in our focus.

Given the breadth and depth of the profession, there are many ways into, of moving within and of transforming a service management career. Whichever industry, you'll find the characteristics and responsibilities of being a service manager similar and therefore transportable. From business relationship management to service and process design; from empathic leadership to customer experience management and more, you'll find that human competencies such as emotional intelligence, knowledge management and an adaptable resilience are crucial to the role.

The value of service management is in the capability of the people to create and manage the service that matches the wanted experiences of the customers and employees, and delivers the desired organisation outcomes."

From a Service Management Practitioner's Perspective

Lucy Grimwade (she/her)
Enterprise Service Management Consultant

"I have often seen service management being referred to as 'IT support'. Although this is only a small part of the practice and lifecycle, we can take that support element as a concept when we explore the usefulness of service management – both as a career path and as an organisational enabler.

Career: *Developing an IT support skill set that includes (but is not limited to) resilience, problem-solving, empathy, interpersonal communication and reactiveness can empower your career within service management. These power skills can expand across all ITSM practices and career paths and ultimately help you drive efficiency, deliver change and develop personal growth into leadership.*

Organisational enabler*: IT support is frequently viewed as a foundation to enable a business to operate, and service management does indeed underpin the entire organisation by enabling people, processes and technology. The value-add function will drive organisations with activities that include increasing productivity, reducing costs and maintaining day-to-day service.*

In the technology-driven world we live in, service management is the essential wrap required to drive businesses forward. The growing and evolving industry offers career security and progression as well as business success and growth."

From a Service Management Expert's Perspective

Matt Beran
Host of Ticket Volume Podcast, InvGate Product Specialist, IT Fan

"Simply put, service management gives all businesses a construct to consider the methods and practices required to deliver services. Every business that delivers a product or service is doing service management, so I guess the value is that it generates revenue for the company and value to those whom they serve."

From a Service Management Expert's Perspective

Claire Agutter
Director at Scopism, Service Management Author and Host of The ITSM Crowd

These words have been reproduced with Claire's permission from an article regarding the use of a service management approach called SIAM (service integration and management). Article located at:

https://www.scopism.com/what-is-service-integration-and-management-siam/.

"Imagine this scenario.

You're accountable for a critical digital business system – let's use the accounts system as an example. You get a phone call in the middle of the night to say that no one can send or receive any payments. Business processes are failing, and the consequences could be huge.

No problem! You call your supplier for the application. That should fix things. But they deny all knowledge of an issue. It must, they suggest, be an infrastructure problem. So, you call the infrastructure team on their out-of-hours number. Not us, they say. Have you tried the security team? We know they were doing some patching last night. The clock is ticking, and you're getting nowhere fast.

This might be a scenario you've already experienced. Businesses are more and more reliant on automated services, and those services are more and more likely to be provided by a complex network of service providers.

Think about how different things could be. In a service management SIAM model, this type of incident would be dealt with collaboratively across all your service providers. With everyone focused on end-to-end service delivery rather than their contractual targets, you will get the outcome you need much more quickly. And, of course, this is just the start of what service management delivered via SIAM can do. Many organisations start from this reactive position, using SIAM to bring some cooperation to their service delivery. But in the longer term, building a collaborative culture across your ecosystem has huge benefits leading to innovation and improvement."

From a Service Management 'Newbie's' Perspective

Gareth Jones
Project Manager with a Background in Business Analysis

"I am a service management newbie. I probably shouldn't be, as having worked in the IT industry for 20 years providing business analysis services for the last 15, you might think I've crossed paths with service management practices before... And it's fair to say that I did, multiple

times. However, armed with what I know now, if I look back, it feels like I was never in an environment with a solid grasp of the service management lifecycle and how to implement this to manage the lifecycle of a digital service effectively.

In the past 15 months or so, I have been deeply entrenched in this world, and one of the biggest things I have learned is that service management does not need to be complicated.

Service management is not just a guide on 'how to support stuff'. It is so much more than that. It really should be the heartbeat of every organisation's digital and tech world. It is useful in multiple ways, but one that jumps out is how it can enable organisations to strategically innovate, deliver and run quality services for their customers."

From a C-level Perspective

Daniel Breston
Retired CIO, now a Public Speaker and Board Member at the itSMF UK

Daniel writes from the perspective of a CIO or principle consultant for a large firm.

"Every business is in the business of managing their services. If they are not doing this, then why do they exist? This can be public or private, but once you create an organisation, you have to manage the people that are managing the products and services that represent you. In this regard, service management is a role and part of every employee's job description, regardless of their level. Add technology, and you can do service management better and more safely.

Faster – hmm, maybe. Depends on what you do. But if you can do better and more safely, faster and for less is an outcome (not a goal).”

From a C-Level Perspective

Suraj Bithal
C-level Executive

“Having sat on various executive boards and committees, I am always keen to observe how many of the execs around the table are focused on the operating side of their business. So many discussions centre around product and business development opportunities, finance operations and organisational issues, but more attention should be paid to service management.

I would consider many areas of service management useful to any management team, such as service stability, service risks and issues, and licensing, among others. Still, to me, as an exec, the metrics and the detail behind the data are crucial to running any business. But maybe I am one of the rare breeds from an operational background, so I appreciate the data and what it tells us. I am talking about those boring tables that are usually pushed to the back of the pack or are in the appendix.

Over the past few years, it is noticeable that executives and leadership teams are becoming more interested in the trending and performance data that service management processes provide and realise this data is fundamental to their decision-making. The science behind these decisions is paramount to the next investment, initiative or business expansion. After all, if performance is going the wrong way, this leads to dissatisfaction, leading to reputational damage.

So why do so many companies ignore the investment in service and metrics? Well, it is common for boards to look at the hard visible costs and not hidden costs, and this is where service management at its best comes to the front.

For example, the costs of an incident or a failed change can be calculated relatively simply, with the correct toolset. These costs give us an insight into operating losses or profit loss at a much more detailed level. The cost of the actual running of a service is something that is rarely requested. Many execs will look at the monthly service charge and ignore the waste.

It is only when the business is unable to operate efficiently or programme costs start to accelerate out of control that leaders start to ask questions and enquire about the quality of tooling and data. Service management is a proactive tool as well as a reactive enabling function.

So, I know service management lets me know that my business is safe or has challenges to deal with, but where service management really adds true value at the top table is in the metrics it provides. An enabling service management function is commonly underinvested in or just misunderstood."

The Author's View

Note to the reader; I made sure to write this chapter and the book as a whole before I asked for my contributors' input; I didn't want to be influenced by their words.

This section was written before receiving the contributions above to answer the question:

What makes service management so valuable?

Digital services are the heart of organisations; every product is a service, and service management is a vital organ in their design and delivery. Technology is nothing without a service wrap; two of the most renowned 'service' organisations are Amazon and Apple, each technology titans.

Both organisations are built upon a clear service strategy and service design ethos. They rely on excellent management practices to fulfil orders and use knowledge management and vendor partnerships to support and deliver their products.

Apple makes the experience of using its products as easy and seamless as possible. Providing omnichannel access to customer support, options that add value as customers troubleshoot issues they encounter with their products, all adding to the 'experience'.

Amazon's mission statement is "to be Earth's most customer-centric company". It recognises that every product is a service and that every service is only as good as its practices, knowledge and partners (to name a few).

Amazon knows that excellent customer service is crucial to achieving this goal. By prioritising the needs and desires of its customers, Amazon builds loyalty, increases customer satisfaction and drives repeat business.

Both companies also recognise the importance of convenience and speed. They offer fast, reliable shipping and easy returns and exchanges, making the online shopping and support experience seamless and helping them become the most popular e-commerce platforms in the world, stealing a march on competitors.

Amazon and Apple use sophisticated algorithms and data analysis to track customer behaviour, identify issues and optimise the customer experience. This allows them to anticipate and address customer needs before they become a problem, resulting in a smoother and more satisfying customer experience.

Both companies empower their teams, using service management fundamentals to influence their whole enterprise. This is why service management is so valuable.

Summary

I had a purpose when inviting the input of professionals working in and around service management and those receiving the benefits of it.

First and foremost, this was to provide a view more rounded than just my own. When I asked for this feedback, these contributors were only provided with an overview of this book as I drafted it. I did not ask for a positive or negative perspective; I did not suggest what they should or could say. They were simply asked, "What makes service management so valuable?

We see genuine views on service management and its value on these pages. Every contributor suggests or remarks on service management as an organisational enabler.

The value of service management is well-known for those of us in the profession. I hope readers looking to build a career in service management will find this compelling, intriguing and motivating. Service management influences and enables organisations at all levels, which means you can too.

You can take this career anywhere in the world, into any industry. In time, work will come to you as you identify reoccurring cross-organisational digital service issues. For as long as IT is a service, you'll have a job as a service management professional.

Service management is a career that will challenge and motivate you in equal measure; it will stretch your capabilities, develop your technical skills, and provide you with a network of professionals who will become more than just colleagues. And without placing too fine a point on it, good service management professionals can earn a fantastic compensation package.

For readers in leadership roles, take onboard what has been said and invite your service management teams into strategic conversations. Link them with your finance, marketing, HR and risk management teams to enable them to deliver co-created value that can save your organisation money, improve your employee productivity, reduce your regulatory risk and costs, improve your velocity in speed to market and enhance your consumer and customer experience.

In the last few years alone, I have worked with organisations where a newly designed and formed service management function has identified and kicked off a process to save hundreds of thousands of pounds in digital service savings, identified and returned hours of productivity to each person in the enterprise, and all of this has reduced costs while improving the experience of consumers and that of multi-billion-pound clients.

Little of this was achieved through technology; it was achieved through gathering the trust of leadership via reliable service management data and process analysis. Savings and productivity were returned through the practice of knowledge management and well-considered management information and reporting, not to mention the great work of a dedicated service management office. In all cases, this value was co-created through conversation, debate and communities of practice (CoPs).[6]

These and everything else within this chapter are just elements of what makes service management valuable. Still, these kinds of results can only be achieved if we work together to enable enterprise service management.

---

[6] *"A community of practice (CoP) is a group of people who share a common concern, a set of problems, or an interest in a topic and who come together to fulfill both individual and group goals."* Source: *https://www.communityofpractice.ca/background/what-is-a-community-of-practice/*.

CHAPTER 5: ENABLING ENTERPRISE SERVICE MANAGEMENT

This chapter is dedicated to those still wondering what enterprise service management is or how to/why put it in place.

Let's ask ourselves the following question.

Is enterprise service management important?

As always, answering the question directly is difficult, but we can walk towards this. Firstly, let's clarify that this is not enterprise service management versus ITSM.

Enterprise service management lifts IT practices into the enterprise as a whole, and the key to enabling this is to 'do with' as opposed to 'do to'. Enterprise service management is developed from and complemented by ITSM and all that has been learned over the last forty years.

Suppose you have implemented or are implementing ITSM. In that case, you are working towards helping your organisation build upon its digital service strategy and contributing to its success in operating those digital services and the organisation's regulatory and reputational status by standardising them via the service lifecycle.

All great stuff, I'm sure you'll agree.

On the other hand, enterprise service management adopts some of those existing ITSM practices, takes on board the lessons learned in the past and applies principles in a way that has been relied on by ITSM experts for many years.

However, moving past ITSM into enterprise service management will require more than just IT teams; you will need to think outside this team and its practices, and you'll need to lead from the front and communicate appropriately, and so much more. We'll cover those elements here.

Organisation leadership and enterprise service management

A recurring theme is that of ITSM teams removing the purely 'IT' aspect of their role and embracing the 'service and management' aspect.

IT remains critical as most companies nowadays are digital, but here's what I've found in my experience…this may be controversial…drum roll… Leaders do not understand IT, and they sure as eggs are eggs do not 'get' enterprise-focused service management.

Of course, that only applies if they've not finished this book ☺

These statements are not intended to cause offence, nor are they factually accurate 100% of the time, but this is my experience. After years of these factors frustrating me and my efforts, I realised a few things:

- Service management is not taught in schools, colleges, universities or even in MBAs. Aspects of it are taught, such as strategic planning, resource planning, project management, development languages, even scientific and analytical approaches. Still, none of it is labelled as service management or ITSM, let alone enterprise service management.

- Organisational leaders must look at many aspects of an organisation; why would they focus on IT or ITSM? They have shareholder accountabilities, press and marketing, regulators, finance, risk management, people, etc.; in most cases, they leave this to trusted staff.
- The same applies to start-ups; they've far too much going on to consider how a service management governance practice can help them as they scale or how a Change enablement process can increase their product and service velocity.
- Service management training is not aimed at C-level or execs. Why would they sit an ITIL® Foundation or VeriSM Foundation course when they have so much else going on? (See "Education in Service Management" section.)

It is part of our job to educate our leaders. Explain to them the benefits of enterprise service management and highlight how it can enable their organisations. Even though it is a cost to them, it can save them money, make them money, protect them from reputational damage and regulatory impact, and improve productivity and digital experiences.

If, as enterprise service management professionals, we explain what we do appropriately, we can convince them to empower enterprise-focused service management to design, deliver, operate and continually improve digital services for the whole enterprise, its customers, consumers and partners!

Of course, this is easier said than done, and it takes confidence to approach your leadership in this way, but a good leader will listen and take note. As I found with my VeriSM elevator pitch as referenced elsewhere in the book.

We as an industry should also join together to make these statements. We are a young industry, but right now, we have a generational group of experts working in ITSM who have picked up these learnings through applying service management across different industries; these people built the industry. Their learned experience and ways of working are so important to educate our leaders on.

Added to this, we have new generations, ideas and beliefs coming into the industry, a generation that has grown up with digital services and sees the need to put digital at the heart of everything we do. These people are not limited to working in ITSM or even IT; they work throughout organisations and realise the benefit of digital enablement as part of their everyday lives. We need to work among these people and spread the benefits of what we do and how it can positively impact them, their careers and their organisations.

Now is the perfect time to achieve a consistent approach to the delivery of digital services as a result of this industry experience and the new wave of digitally-led employees and consumers. This can be achieved through the correct level of education and cross-pollination of skills and ideas as part of a drive to co-create value across organisations and, indeed, across organisational and geographical boundaries.

We need to influence educational and private examining bodies as well as professional bodies and organisations to work together to ensure that ITSM is both accessible from an educational standpoint and usable from an organisational perspective. In an ideal world, we can then better demonstrate the benefits of ITSM to senior business leaders such that they can invite service management to the table as they strategise the development of enterprise-focused service management and their organisational goals.

For me, a key to this is education to all involved in our industry and especially to the decision makers at C-level who currently need a viable entry point to formal ITSM qualifications and education. We must remedy this, and I see a book such as this one, our industry podcasts and webinars, and our communities, plus working across the likes of ISO as a way to achieve this.

Wherever we can, we need to work with our leaders to promote enterprise-level service management as they are in a perfect position to collaborate among their peers and with their knowledge of the bottom line, business strategy and objectives. They can see when the organisation is ready, willing and able to accept significant change or iterations, and detect early signs that some departments may pose objections.

As with any change, there are many reasons – ranging from a fear of negative consequences to compliance with a top-down culture – why some senior leaders might not be willing to voice their ideas and become the champions for enterprise-based service management.

This is not a quick process, but the following are just a few techniques that can help you overcome the challenges.

- **Appropriate messaging:** Tailor your messaging to make enterprise-based service management sound more appealing to 'sell' your ideas to C-level executives. You must familiarise yourself with your C-level's unique blend of goals, values and knowledge, and allow that insight to shape your message. Often it also pays to leave out words like 'ITIL', 'Process' and 'Governance', and focus on how you enable the organisation. If the members of your C-level are bottom-line focused, then demonstrate how an enterprise-focused service management function reduces costs by reducing critical digital incidents and improving service quality and employee productivity. All of these impact the bottom line.

- **Highlight why enterprise service management is good:** Whether the function itself or its benefits appear on your company's list of priorities depends on how you package them. Sponsoring an enterprise service management function might seem like a high-cost, low-benefit idea to some C-level people until you explain how it supports one of their corporate goals – like increasing customer satisfaction, improving colleague productivity or improving digital speed to market.
  Then, suddenly, your idea sounds more feasible and appealing to them. Once they see how your initiative fits into the company's big picture, they will be more willing to devote resources to it and support it via the appropriate communication channels.
- **Involve other people** – If it's been said once in this book, it's been said a thousand times here and elsewhere; build a community of like-minded people. Building a community focused on value generates organisational buy-in faster and on a larger scale because more people contribute energy and resources to your cause. For example, one person might have access

to essential data, while another might have a better relationship with one of the C-level executives you are trying to persuade. Invite the C-level exec to your community, let them see what you are doing, and have others extol the benefits.

- **Use proof-of-concept solutions** – Coming up with a community-led, innovative proof-of-concept suggestion is a great way to get the ball rolling.
  Discuss your proof of concept, the challenge it aims to address and the value it will add; you could call it a proposal.
  Be sure to include specific details that concentrate on how you plan to deliver value in line with the strategic intent and company vision. Where possible, highlight relevant aspects such as potential cost savings or improved customer experience (possibly both) and illustrate how this will be measured and shared over a defined period. From here, do the following:
  - **Identify quick wins**: If there is a service that is continually failing or a process/practice that is not adding value, use your community to build an iterative solution to use to measure the failing process as is and then measure the improvement made iteratively. You can then use this proof-of-concept evidence to promote enterprise service management practices and scale up as appropriate.
  - **Be clear on your needs**: It's incredibly important that the service management professional or team is aware of the empowerment and support that their

leadership will offer. Support can be offered in many forms. So often you'll hear "tell me what you need"; my advice would be to ask for communication and support as well as budget. Prepare the communications on behalf of your leadership team or get an angle into your internal communications team or marketing so you can efficiently communicate your clear messages.

- Prepare communication and messaging to send to your stakeholders using as many channels as possible, but ask that your leadership either send or publicly endorse these messages. If your company has a 'town hall' or 'quarterly announcement', seek a spot on this and have your leadership endorse what you are saying. If others see this level of support, your job will be a little easier.

The enterprise service management office

At this point, it's good to take a step back and consider the mechanics of delivering a great enterprise-wide service management function. For me, the organisation of this business-enabling function is delivered via a service management office (SMO).

An enterprise SMO (referred to hereafter as 'SMO' for simplicity), is a team that should be set up to function as a centre of excellence for enterprise-focused service management, ensuring continual development, improvement and knowledge management that delivers a consistent application of management practices across the enterprise.

Given that service management is a *"Service management is a set of specialized organizational capabilities for providing value to customers in the form of services,"*[7] the SMO helps the organisation develop these capabilities into an enterprise-enabling function.

The image shows a typical service management office that works across the enterprise at operational, tactical and strategic levels. It will cover the digital service lifecycle from service strategy through to service operation and continual improvement. Additionally, *the service management office collaborates with the project management office (PMO) where one exists, to align project outcomes with service quality, ensuring seamless transition and ongoing operational excellence.*

This is not the de-facto standard for a service management office; it is more a way of illustrating the breadth of responsibility and accountability a service management office can deliver to the enterprise as a whole.

[7] *https://www.greycampus.com/opencampus/itil-foundation/service-management-as-a-practice.*

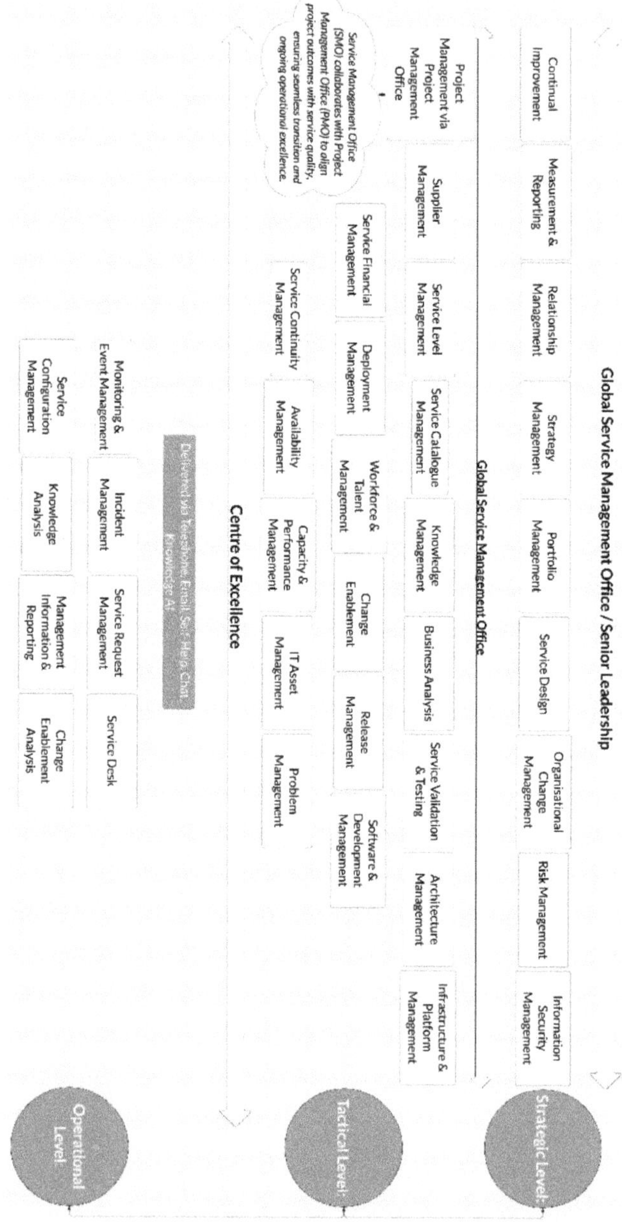

Figure 3: Example Service Management Office Accountabilities

An SMO can take several forms, which depend upon the organisation and its strategic intent and objectives for service management and its role within the enterprise. An SMO can be formalised and drive service management throughout the enterprise and into partners, or it can be less formal with teams focused on the continual development of the organisation's management practices.

A big challenge for any SMO is that the 'governance' can be viewed negatively in some organisations or by team members within these organisations. It's often because of misapplication of service management governance (such as my own in the past) and similar behaviour that a negative perception can be built.

Therefore, it's essential to frame your SMO launch and the operational communications appropriately, focusing on enterprise enablement. An SMO can play an important role in breaking down bureaucracy and ensuring that policies and controls are right-sized as appropriate to the organisation, its customers, consumers and partners – not to mention the regulators. An SMO can also help distinguish between controls that are necessary to satisfy legal and regulatory requirements and internal controls that can be adapted.

An SMO and its members wear many hats, which adds variety and hopefully relieves boredom. As well as governance, practices and service operation, an SMO can monitor the performance and conformance of activities against the strategic and tactical direction of the enterprise. It can continually evaluate those activities to ensure that they are appropriate to the enterprise and its circumstances, its needs, strategic goals, tactical aims and operational challenges.

This is especially important. As an enterprise enabler and a way of altering the perception of a 'governance only' function, a well-designed, empowered SMO can work across the enterprise to accelerate the organisation's digital transformation initiatives. It can enable the velocity of product development and innovation efforts, and enhance customer experience through improving reliability and turning a cost function into a revenue-making function. Another awesome benefit of an SMO is the ability to leverage and adapt established best practices and turn these into a common language that the whole organisation can use; the SMO can share its understanding of concepts, which in turn will bring others on the journey.

A key SMO function and a key element of the digital service lifecycle is the culture of continual improvement. Using practices such as a value-focused CoP (community of practice) and running these from the SMO can enable interactions and listening to colleagues, customers, consumers and partners in delivering enterprise service management solutions.

A well-run and empowered SMO can build a culture of continual learning and improvement, returning us to the enterprise service management principles discussed elsewhere: continual experimentation, controlled risks and learning from failure.

Enterprise service management office and strategies

To effectively deliver management practices, governance and thought leadership, those working in the SMO must commit themselves to ensure they are continually learning and improving, and willing to share what they learn!

This involves being clear on the organisation's strategy and influencing it wherever possible using service management practices and your own experience across industries to make this enterprise-focused.

To be an enterprise function, the SMO must align with the organisation's strategic vision and goals, so team members must be well-versed in this area. Another real bonus is looking from the outside in, using your customers' perspective as a starting point, as well as gathering industry knowledge and professional knowledge and an understanding of trends that are impacting, disrupting and enabling the industry. This enables the SMO to adapt strategies to assist with product digital-service innovation.

Identifying and learning about relevant best practices, frameworks and guiding principles is important; this understanding should be used to challenge the status quo and any strategic intent. This is not to be difficult; it's to constructively critique the strategy and those actions underway or planned to deliver them.

No one framework is perfect, and several of them can be blended to deliver the desired strategy; members of the SMO must learn about and align relevant ways of working, becoming masters in how to 'adopt and adapt' and then apply this across the enterprise using continual improvement.

From both a strategic and tactical level, the SMO is ideally positioned to mentor and coach teams on how to improve continually, and wherever possible, these activities should be aligned to strategy to help with buy-in. This means that members need to learn about and practice principles-based ways of working along with proven methods and techniques.

Enterprise service management delivery principles

ITSM is incredibly effective in improving an organisation's performance, efficiency, receptiveness and ability to evaluate its success.

Enterprise service management must do more than duplicate the existing ITSM principles, especially if you are pulling those from a textbook; every organisation is different.

Enterprise-focused service management must adopt and adapt these principles to meet each organisational element and partner's unique needs. An objective of adopting these principles is to ensure that everyone in your organisation speaks the same language and has full access to the necessary support promptly and consistently.

Here are some of the main enterprise service management principles to guide you when embedding such a practice within your enterprise.

Efficiency: A well-designed and operated enterprise service management platform and associated SMO should be able to enhance your enterprise, ensuring that your delivery and acceptance of digital services are efficient and continually improving.

When all incidents and requests are directed to your service desk, they should land to the intended team or individual directly; if they do not, this should be subject to continual knowledge management that closes gaps and improves quality and productivity. Doing this ensures that every customer, consumer and colleague interaction handled via your team is handled effectively on the first contact. With streamlined service delivery, your enterprise will minimise time wastage and ensure better efficiency in all departments.

Knowledge accessibility: By implementing enterprise service management for knowledge management, you'll ensure that all team members have direct paths to information without relying on other members of the organisation.

This improvement in accessibility effectively improves colleague productivity and effectiveness because they don't have to waste time going through various departments to access the information they need.

If you can, focus on developing an accessible and sustainable tool governed centrally in your SMO and available for everyone in the enterprise, from marketing to people and culture to CEOs. Doing this will further enable self-service and self-education and improve the experience of interacting with your service management teams.

Simplicity: Many believe that the design and operation of IT are complicated, but it does not need to be.

New enterprise-focused service management programmes should improve and modernise the colleague, customer and consumer experience. Identifying and co-creating these advancements as a 'value' will be beneficial for everyone across the organisation and deliver enterprise-wide benefits.

IT specialists and, indeed, your colleagues want to solve problems at work with the same degree of flexibility they enjoy at their leisure. With value as a focus, you can co-create, design and deliver simplicity to your organisation via elements such as a self-service technology option that uses knowledge management to allow your colleagues, customers and consumers to self-service their requirements and your team to work on innovative value-focused solutions. Doing this increases your employees' will to work, improving your colleague, customer and consumer satisfaction, experience and productivity. In many cases, this will also reduce costs over time, providing a return on investment within approximately 18 months.

Optimisation and automation: Once you reduce waste, make knowledge accessible and implement a simple value-focused technology solution, you can seek to automate the processes in your organisation.

Doing so helps reduce instances of guesswork and human errors in your enterprise, which can easily result in financial and productivity losses. Optimising essential processes can reduce waste and potentially reduce touch points and potential breaks or chances of broken data sets. Once this is complete, you can automate previously laborious process work. A great example is a one-step joiners' or leavers' process, thus reducing the chances of broken data and vastly improving the onboarding experience of hiring managers and new joiners. Maybe you, too, will see your organisation on one of those 'look what I got' new joiner experience posts on LinkedIn.

We've always done it this way…

One of the great pleasures of working in service management is our professional ability and need to move between organisations and industries. It provides us with a fantastic view of business and makes us so incredibly interesting at dinner parties ☺.

It also means that you enter organisations and industries that are new to you, and often, you are employed because there is an issue or a series of obstacles to overcome. Every organisation is different, but if I had a pound for every time

I've heard the following phrase, I wouldn't be writing a book about it on a cold Friday in January. That phrase is:

"We've always done it this way."

This is often obstacle number one when entering a new organisation, and it applies as much in sales, marketing, finance, etc., as it does in IT and enterprise service management.

I'd go as far as saying it's also not an entirely ridiculous statement to make, as it makes sense to refine, practice and embed one methodology and work it through.

However, this only works if you constantly seek to evolve and employ your methodology, focusing on enterprise value and enablement. To do this, you might need to pivot and work across more than one way of working. This means taking the way you've always done it and viewing it through the lens of your customer. Do they think it's working? If you even hesitate to answer positively, you must consider how to improve it.

Working across methodologies

As we make our way through life and this book, we'll discuss 'how' and 'why' we do things. It may be our method to poach an egg – boil the water, add olive oil, spin the water, and drop the egg in for two and a half minutes – perfection when served on buttered toast with a little spicy sauce.

My method is the best method out there – for me. It's not for me to suggest your method is better or worse, but we can surely learn from each other. Enterprise service management is no different. Many 'methods' exist, but why not learn from others as opposed to limiting yourself to one?

This is just one of several reasons why the importance of co-creating value and enterprise-focused service management cannot be exaggerated. If done well, it can stimulate organisational growth, so as in life or breaking eggs, there is no 'golden rule'.

There are several guidelines that have evolved over the years and address different business requirements, but there is no straightforward answer to the conundrum of which of these is the 'best practice'. Any answer requires deep thought within your organisation, and it depends upon your exact requirements from a strategic, tactical and enablement point of view. It should, wherever possible, align with your organisational culture and values, as well as how receptive your organisation and its people are to change.

In truth, it is not necessary to choose just one approach; in fact, I'd make the opposite recommendation. You should mix and match different methodologies to address your various requirements, and indeed, that is the only way to get your entire enterprise's service management right and in line with those strategic and value-led requirements.

Simply applying ITIL or any other 'model' in singularity and out of the book is counterproductive; it stimulates your applying a single layer of service management that is merely a book-based approach.

If you do this, you'll lead yourselves down a path where your methodology is not in line with your objectives; as time evolves and your organisation evolves, you'll be completely out of step and potentially disable your enterprise instead of enabling it.

Enterprise service management is not a project to complete, it has no end date, and it must live as part of your organisation, enabling it through taking an iterative and pragmatic approach that looks at the needs of your colleagues, customers, consumers and partners.

You can embed your ways of working or your 'methodologies' and use iterative and continual improvement to introduce complimentary methodologies – don't get stuck in a rut.

"That's a stupid question"

Have you ever heard this before, or have you felt like you'd get this response if you have a question to ask? You're not alone. I have that fear, too; I expect we all do at some point.

In an upcoming section, we will ask, "What makes a great service management professional?" Having been in 'the game' for 30-odd years, one strength I see in good service management people and good leaders is a child-like curiosity. If we are not curious, I struggle to see how we learn.

As service management professionals, we operate across a spectrum of technologies, various organisational departments, partners, customers and consumers; each of these areas works to their own beat, pursuing its own goals and using methodologies; each of them is continually evolving and adding to this heady mix. Our world and everything within it is continually changing.

We cannot be expected to understand all these elements perfectly all of the time, and from an enterprise perspective, we also need to be aware of how they all hang together to enable our organisations continually.

Speaking for myself, I'm not academically 'intelligent', and my wife will tell you I lack common sense in some of the simplest matters; therefore, I must ask questions, and yes, those questions may sometimes be regarded (even by me) as stupid.

A mentee of mine recently asked, "Do you suffer from imposter syndrome?" – Oh yes, I do.

As the years have gone on, I've dampened the imposter syndrome to a whisper at times, but it's still there – and it used to stop me from asking questions. As a result, I stopped learning and began making things up.

It was only when my imposter syndrome faded away that I realised that my childlike curiosity to ask questions was so useful, and in the meantime, my listening skills and ability to process and retain information had improved – a vital ingredient in this mix.

As my experience increased, I learned that one of the great things about working in a variety of industries is the relationships you make and the education every single client and opportunity offers; this opens up the mind to different avenues of achieving great results, which helps propel you in a direction that is both challenging and comforting. But you only do this by asking a question and taking on board the answers.

The futurist Alvin Toffler wrote:

> ***"The illiterate of the 21st century will not be those who cannot read and write, but those who cannot learn, unlearn, and relearn."***[8]

[8] Alvin Toffler, *Future Shock*, (2022). Bantam Books, originally published by Random House, (1970).

I've reflected on this before, but I was first presented with this statement when meeting with a gentleman named Johann Botha. Johann is a digital transformation strategy, change and innovation leader and someone I look up to and admire as both a teacher, a consultant and a person who challenges the norm and challenged my way of thinking.

I was sitting in one of Johann's training sessions, and I had a question that I prefaced with:

"I'm sorry if this is a stupid question". "Here,"* Johann stated, *"no question is stupid".

Rather than this being a throwaway phrase to make me feel better, Johann said this with meaning. He went on to explain that letting go of the old and adopting the new isn't always easy.

Johann introduced me to the *'learn, unlearn, relearn'* statement and put it into context, explaining that we need to learn, unlearn and relearn to keep pace with the rapidly changing world and technology, not to mention world events or political events that impact our continued abilities to trade or indeed expand or disrupt existing or new markets.

As our conversation continued, we discussed how he, I and those present in the room had to keep reinventing ourselves as digital professionals and that this also applies to our teams and the digital services they and we develop and support, as these must not only evolve with our customers but hopefully evolve to create a new consumer demand or disrupt our industries and markets.

There is only one constant as a service management professional: change

Change is the only constant. The only way to keep up with this reality is to learn, unlearn and relearn; this comes with asking questions – stupid or not.

At the start of our careers or education, most of us are excited and keen to learn new things, but with time, we lose interest. We tend to hold on to whatever we learn and work relentlessly without focusing on the need to develop. We stop asking questions and make assumptions. These assumptions are often well-placed, but they can be incorrect due to change.

Resisting the process of unlearning and relearning can hurt our professional growth or the evolution of our business. Therefore, continual improvement and the organisational ability to continually evaluate where we are now and where we want to go should ideally become a fabric of the organisation's culture, or the organisation risks standing still – also known as 'going backwards'.

By asking questions, unlearning and relearning, we can revamp our services and evolve our knowledge to keep pace with the rapidly changing world. By not standing still and letting go of conventional routines, we can challenge ourselves and our organisations to improve continually and provide a level of empowerment to our teams to follow this path.

All this said, you still have a recipient to your questions, and it's how you frame them that can change their response from "that's a stupid question" to "that's an interesting question".

It's important to read the room and try to reach an understanding of how to pitch your question. You may want to consider if your question will lead to a follow-on question and whether this is the right place to have that conversation. You might also wonder just how many questions are too many.

It really does depend on the scenario, but if you are working with a customer or potential service consumer, it's likely that not asking the question can lead to errors, mistakes, conflicts, assumptions, and all manner of ill-feeling that can be costly in time and money for your organisation and its customers and consumers as you'll poorly design a service that will ultimately fail.

Not asking questions can ruin teamwork, individual relationships, projects and deadlines, and result in an unmotivated and uninspired workplace. Without fostering a culture that is open to curiosity, no organisation can innovate successfully.

When I first speak to an organisation, I ask two questions, and these questions remain on the tip of my tongue for the whole engagement and beyond.

Question 1 is:

"What are the organisation's strategic goals?"

By asking this question, I am seeking to understand that person's perception of the organisation's strategy and direction of travel. We usually elaborate on how close the organisation is to achieving these goals or the challenges it is facing in doing so. From here, we dive into the person's contribution towards these goals, their team's contribution, and the relationships they hold in striving towards these goals.

If you ask more than one person this question, you may also find a set of different and possibly even conflicting answers. Having this information enables you to understand if everyone is pulling in the same direction and if the leadership team provides conflicting, opposed or different answers to one another. You can also evaluate if these messages are leading their teams in opposite directions. You can learn a lot from this question.

Question 2:

"What does value mean to you?"

Some people answer this question in a similar vein to "What are the organisation's strategic goals?", which is fine. Others discuss their personal values and how they like to interact with others to meet these values. Asking this question can help you understand the person, what drives them, what motivates them and what demotivates them. It also allows you to share your own values and potentially build a common bond that is not entirely work-related.

Asking this question also provides an insight into the organisational culture that may not be on the organisation's web pages; you see how people may or may not fit in as well as providing conversation and exploring how you could work together on the programme in hand to deliver value to one another as well as meet the organisation's strategic goals.

Most pertinently, as a service management professional, asking these questions allows you to build a picture of what a possible value-focused CoP may look like, who may want to join you, whether this person could be an impactor or influencer, how they'll interact, and what value we can add to the organisation and one another via the community.

If I feel it's right, and after reading the room, I may well ask a third question:

"Would you like to join a value-focused CoP?"

Joining a value-focused CoP should be a choice, and asking these questions gives you a more reasonable chance of attracting the right people who can help you make a difference.

These are the two to three core questions that I use in a lot of my first meetings. I'd love to say that asking the questions gets easier and feels less stupid. It doesn't, but your ability to read the room, the situation and the setting does improve with time, and you are therefore less likely to be seen as asking a stupid question.

To close this section, I'd like to ask two more things of you.

One: Next time you want to ask a question and you think it's stupid, remember this. Somebody else is probably thinking the same thing, so ask the question to help both of you.

Two: You may get asked a question in the future and your colleague, customer, etc. may preface this with: *"This might be a stupid question but..."* Please begin your answer by acknowledging there is no such thing as a stupid question. There's only the stupidity of NOT asking the question. You'll reassure them and help them feel much more comfortable.

Curiosity might have killed the cat but asking the question and learning something new might just lead to something amazing. So please rekindle that childlike curiosity that is so important in service management. If someone asks you a question, check your inner voice for an unhelpful response, and ask yourself instead why you respond that way and how you could reply more positively to give the person what they need.

Is enterprise service management important?

I'm hoping that we've clearly illustrated that none of this works if it's implemented as IT doing it 'to' the business or IT practices being used by the business.

If I have not been clear enough already, this is IT and service management working with the organisation, their colleagues, customers, consumers and partners to discuss, agree and co-create value-based ways of working that are appropriate for the organisation and its strategic and tactical goals. That's enterprise-focused service management.

It should work to align the services your organisation delivers with the overall goals and objectives of the business. By working together and co-creating an understanding of the needs and priorities of the organisation, effective enterprise service management can ensure that services are tailored to support the organisation in reaching its goals and value-focused outcomes.

Used well, enterprise service management can assist in ensuring that resources are being used effectively and that the digital services provided are truly beneficial to the organisation, its employees, customers, consumers and partners.

Another benefit of an enterprise approach to service management is its emphasis on standardisation. Aiming to implement consistent, repeatable and measurable processes and procedures enables the organisation to deliver services in a more predictable and cost-efficient manner.

ITSM is often seen as a cost; standardisation, as used in enterprise service management, can alter this perception, effectively leading to cost savings as once you have standardised elements of your operation, you can automate and incrementally optimise those processes over time.

Working across the organisation using enterprise service management introduces and blends the concepts and value-led outcomes of continual improvement. This is achieved through regular monitoring, measurement and evaluation of the services provided. Working together encourages the co-creation of value as the organisation identifies improvement areas. This co-creation of continual improvement and its ongoing measurement helps to ensure that services are improving in line with the desires of all parties operating and consuming the services.

Summary

In this chapter, we've covered several perspectives in discussing how we may enable enterprise-focused service management, starting from the assumption that we have some form of ITSM in place.

We live in a world that is fast-paced and constantly evolving; my challenge to you is that there is rarely anywhere more fast-paced than IT. You may feel that your ITSM function is immature and couldn't possibly be lifted to an enterprise-focused service management practice, but I would suggest that if you've got digital services up and running, have a service design process in place and you're managing digital services and their delivery to an enterprise – you are perfectly positioned to move from ITSM towards enterprise service management.

Although IT is fast-paced, legislation and working practices rarely keep up with that pace, and this is where we in IT can enable the enterprise. We have to work at pace, constantly be on the verge of innovation, and we must protect our organisations while doing so; the lessons we learn here can be used to enable other critical business functions from the enterprise perspective.

I once had a COO say to me:

"We don't need to assess our IT services; they are all bad; we are starting from zero."

In a way, he was right, but on a much more fundamental level, he was incorrect.

In this case, I could clearly see that people were using PCs and working on Wi-Fi in the office. I was presenting to the COO using a video conferencing platform, and I could observe Kanban boards being used outside.[9] Obviously, we were not starting from zero, but we were starting from a perception of zero, which would be the first thing we'd need to tackle.

To do this, we'd need the support of this very person; we'd need leadership support.

---

[9] A Kanban board is an Agile project management tool designed to help visualise work, limit work-in-progress, and maximise efficiency (or flow).

It would be best if you had this level of support to begin your journey; you can gather this through appropriate messaging and 'selling' your goals and principles. There will be plenty you do right and plenty you can improve. Still, you can only improve these things if you work with your stakeholders, business partners, colleagues, customers and consumers to measure what's going well. Looking at the whole enterprise with an outside-in view, it is here that you will lift yourselves from ITSM to 'ESM', as enterprise service management is sometimes called.

Clearly define and communicate your strategic and tactical goals, articulate your principles and measure your progress. Ensure that you are using the relevant blend of methodologies and do not be scared to ask 'stupid questions' while you must also understand that no question is stupid in itself.

Once you've set yourself on this path, you must also bring as many others as you can on this journey – do not work in isolation. If you want to achieve great things, you'll need to measure your successes with as many stakeholders as possible; this is where communication and community can help you.

CHAPTER 6: SERVICE MANAGEMENT COMMUNICATION AND COMMUNITY

Strong communication is of great importance in enterprise service management. It has the power to drive you towards your goals and value-focused outcomes successfully by improving collaborative practices and holistic working, all while promoting transparency and building trusting relationships.

Throughout this book, I explain that my approach has, at times, been built more around governance than it was around collaborative communication. This was a great failing of mine, and if I'm honest, I continue to see others working this way on plenty of my engagements.

Our ability to communicate using multiple methods is the key skill of a great service management professional. Communication can benefit you in so many ways, and some principles of doing so are now key components of the various service management practices and methodologies.

As part of running an IT service, I like to develop a series of communication plans for that service; it is key to holistic working. To do this, I work with my customers, colleagues and vendors to identify all the key stakeholder groups involved in delivering a service. Through understanding this, you can build a more holistic view of the service. By defining how you will communicate to stakeholder groups, customers, colleagues and vendors from the outset, you can avoid issues during the service lifecycle; you can also take 'temperature checks' regularly and benefit from all parties being on the same page.

A comprehensive communication plan should detail the channels used and the frequency of communication. It should also take into account using the right communication for the right audiences.

An example would be a process used to report an incident on a digital service. Process and policy documents are necessities to operate and support services, but they should also be living documents that are reviewed with stakeholders and amended over time. That said, sometimes you can simplify this activity by turning seemingly complex process steps into pictures that enable a speedier review for all parties and allow you to communicate more clearly to those with no interest in the process outside of their part of interacting with it.

This investment of time and effort into communication planning is well worth it. Good and well-considered communication has the power to influence the attitudes of your customers, your teams and your partners. It can help bring teams together and ensure smooth, holistic working across departments and ecosystems.

This filters right down to jargon and terminology. Work with all your stakeholders to ensure you have consistent language across the board; this is proven to prevent issues of miscommunication.

The scenario I gave in the "Service Management Reporting – and Influencing" section is a real case in point. Good service management relies on coordinating activities, working as one and strong communication, which is paramount to achieving success.

To enable the achievement of fantastic digital service delivery, teams must work collaboratively. Collaborative working is easier said than done, especially in today's world of tight deadlines and raging fires, where digital and information technology services fail; it's at these points that the calm head of a service management professional is so useful.

Outside of these events, teams and individuals tend to work in a siloed manner. Recent remote working arrangements as prompted by the COVID-19 pandemic have in some ways increased these siloed activities as more people work away from the office. On the plus side, and as a result of the pandemic, teams are beginning to move towards transparent ways of working. Wherever possible, service management professionals should promote and elevate this collaborative culture.

Being a good communicator goes deeper than the surface level. It breaks down boundaries, builds relationships and instils trust, all of which is vitally important in those moments when something breaks at 3 am on a public holiday, and you need to mobilise a team to restore the service. At these times, those customers, employees and stakeholders know they can rely on your communications, as well as trust in you to understand their key outcomes in restoring service.

Transparency is also key to delivering enterprise-wide service management. In terms of customer relations, while it may be the job of the marketing or sales teams to promote the business, the people and culture teams to engage new employees or retain existing employees, it is when working holistically that enterprise-focused service management professionals and service management departments also have a role to play. Every point of communication with a customer, potential customer, client or stakeholder should work to instil trust in your company.

Of course, communication is a two-way and continual thing. Asking, listening, observing and empathising (ALOE) go a long way to building trust with your stakeholders. They are a key element of enterprise-focused service management, as is acting upon this feedback and using it to evolve both yourself and improving your services continually.

Acting upon this feedback is vital, as is taking sustainable steps through progressing iteratively; taking giant leaps is only sometimes necessary. Making improvements and taking the time to onboard feedback can help you progress. This agile way of working allows you to make changes and adapt accordingly while always validating your direction.

When designing or reviewing your digital service, encourage and include plenty of periodic opportunities for feedback from all stakeholders, especially your customers and consumers. Meet with all relevant parties before making any changes based on this feedback, and be sure to keep communication with your teams transparent to obtain buy-in. And always, always measure and report on your success or those hurdles you face; not communicating these can destroy trust quickly.

I hope, at this point, you'll have seen how service management professionals are pivotal to ensuring all communications are handled appropriately within their services. However, why stop there? Service management can impact whole enterprises, and it's from here we'll discuss the concepts of organisational change and of building communities.

Service management and organisational change

Service management is endorsed through various training programmes and certifications; these are necessities that enable organisations and professionals to baseline their skills, but these are only some of the be-all and end-all to being a great enterprise-focused service management professional. It's not just what you know, but how you apply what you know, that makes you great and a valued asset in enabling the organisation.

Personal qualities, accredited skills and the ability to understand and, in some ways, transform elements of organisational culture contribute to creating a successful enterprise service management function that continually co-creates and delivers value-focused outcomes in line with and contributing to strategic organisational goals.

We now work in a world where skills and cultural behaviours have become broader – we are no longer pigeonholed as specialists. People are hungry and indeed need to be learning continually and adapting. We rarely stay in the same lane throughout our careers; service management offers the ability to work across industries and sectors. I have worked in the following industries either as an employee or as an outsourced supplier, and I will attempt to tell you in chronological order, as below.

- Three-person IT company: 1993–1994
- The motor trade: 1994–1997
- Retail: 1997–1998
- Petroleum, oils and chemicals: 1998–1999
- Telecommunications: 1999–2001
- Finance: 2001–2002

- UK Government: 2003–2005
- Finance: 2005–2008
- UK Government: 2008–2012
- Mobile communications: 2012–2013
- Transport: 2013–2014
- Cloud technology: 2014
- Artificial intelligence: 2015
- Education: 2015–2019
- Retail banking and wealth management: 2019–2020
- Networks and data Centres: 2020
- Tobacco: 2020–2021
- Travel, tourism, insurance: 2021–2023
- Banking: 2023
- Energy: 2023

Highlighting the industries I've worked in is designed to show you just how many industries you can work in and the level of experience you can obtain when operating in ITSM.

IT is everywhere; we've discussed how it weaved its way into our lives. That said, IT also impacts ways of working, and this is why a service management professional's ability to be empathetic is vital to success.

Working in ITSM lends itself to having a diverse set of skills; these will be discussed in greater depth elsewhere in this book; in brief, and as per any role, organisations need a good balance of people with the skillsets and capabilities across competencies to enable effective service management and greater maturity.

We have also discussed ALOE (asking, listening, observing and empathising). Each one of the attributes within ALOE and especially empathy is a vital element for the service management professional; our role often involves understanding and empathising with the interests of others by placing ourselves in their shoes. To do this needs a certain amount of emotional intelligence to empathise with others working in different business functions. This can be achieved through asking, listening and observing to allow you to build a sufficient understanding of your colleagues', customers' and consumers' needs.

As per my time working on the service desk, for me being a great service management professional is about helping others enable their day-to-day activities through the delivery of fantastic digital ITSM. In an industry that's existed for approximately 40 years, it's odd to speak of our role in a 'traditional' sense, but the vast majority of service management professionals have indeed originated from an IT function, be that service desk, engineer, developer – we tend to see things from that perspective as opposed to from the colleague, customer or consumer perspective.

Our approach often requires a shift in mindset: it's less about fixing a PC or application – we need to shift from closing the ticket and moving on or reporting on the past. It's more about how we consider our colleagues, customers and consumers and their experience of service and the value-focused outcomes they need to accomplish – which relates back to how we apply true enterprise-focused service management.

We, as an enterprise function, can work with our organisational leadership teams to inform and influence strategy; added to this, we can help with the enterprise direction and culture by taking a much more empathetic view and through designing, operating and continually improving digital IT services through taking a view of our colleagues', customers' and consumers' journeys from their perspective.

By aligning ourselves with organisational leadership and building communities, we can take an innovative approach to develop the ideas and skills of tomorrow throughout our ecosystem, with a solid foundation of leadership empowering a culture change.

Doing so demands a clear picture of why and what's in it for the people involved and the organisation. This is where our service management professionals' communication, influencing and presentation skills are key to presenting the rationale for change. We need to be strategic in our thinking and prepared to take iterative steps while continually seeking feedback. We need to operate across organisations, showing our colleagues, customers, consumers and partners the value attached to the outcome of change.

Ultimately, we must work on being part of the solution and evolution of organisational and cultural change, working across the organisation to empower people to be part of the change and move away from 'doing to' to 'co-creating value'. Once we do this, we will be able to gather ideas and innovate in previously unknown ways using the expertise of our colleagues, customers, consumers and partners.

We can achieve this in several ways, via surveys, service reviews and feedback, but actions speak louder than words in this case. In the next section, we'll discuss how service management professionals can empower themselves and others to take action and co-create value across the organisation to stimulate organisational change via the creation of service and value-focused CoPs (communities of practice).

Co-creating enterprise value with CoPs

We've discussed how valuable service management is, what makes a great service management professional and some of the most important elements of service management. None of that matters if others are unaware of its relevance and importance.

I'm biased, but I think service management is a true organisational enabler. I feel like I've always had that view, but what's certain to me is that over the last few years, the concept of 'enterprise service management' has grown, and it's a subject of some debate.

Enterprise service management is the extension of ITSM principles. Its aim is to enable improved delivery of digital and business services for enterprise enablers like the people and culture teams, marketing teams, legal teams and finance teams. Essentially, it's about co-creating value and enabling the whole enterprise to use IT to deliver end-to-end IT and digital services to employees, customers and consumers of services.

While other departments such as the people and culture and marketing teams have offered internal 'services', they've rarely applied the structure and frameworks offered in ITSM. Enterprise service management is achieved through using all that ITSM good practices have learned over the last 40–50 years and enabling whole organisations through sharing what we've learned.

It was not too long ago that IT was consigned to the basement and seen as somewhat of dark art, a situation where only the IT department understood how to exploit IT. However, we now live in a digital age where the vast majority of people conceptually understand how digital IT services improve and enable our day-to-day lives.

Therefore, those of us who work in the IT sector and service management sub-sector must combine our expertise with that of our network of colleagues and customers to co-create real value in the design and delivery of enterprise-wide service management.

I've heard it said before that, at its heart, good service management is built upon educated experimentation. As a collective, we have developed to a level where education, experience, membership and an educated opinion are highly valued. Much of this is thanks to our certification in management practices and frameworks. In addition, we also rely on our experiences to inform our decisions. This is often referred to as 'adopt and adapt'. The adoption, adaptation and optimisation of ITSM within our organisations is something that is often positively encouraged – but how do we extend this approach to the co-creation of value throughout an organisation?

Over the years, I have worked in teams where we do things 'to' customers. We'd set up policies, processes and measurements and facilitate workshops where we'd tell our customers how to work, what to measure when to meet, etc. This worked well, to a degree. Programmes were signed off and invoices were settled, but what difference did we make? Had we co-created value or just done 'IT' to our customers?

Since working as a consultant in enterprise-focused service management, I've had to find a new way of doing things. Thanks to some remarkable customers and colleagues, I've been able to adopt and adapt the co-creation of value as opposed to doing things 'to' them.

How? One way is to create value-focused CoPs.

Establishing a value-focused CoP

Over the last few years, I have set up and run several value-focused CoPs. Over time, these have grown into other value-focused communities within organisations, even developing into CoPs that sit across our industry and focus on career progression, mentoring and the improvement of IT careers for women.

My first time implementing a CoP was when I was working on the improvement of digital service quality across a global finance organisation. This organisation had identified that silos had developed across its digital teams, geographies and technologies, and further investigation indicated that these were proving disruptive in delivering real service quality to both the internal users, key customers and consumers, and ultimately diminishing the digital service experience, which was driving customers to their competitors.

I worked as part of a team of service management experts from several backgrounds; working together, we discovered a current state where digital front-end services were developing at a pace in line with the client's vision and strategy; seemingly, this was perfect. Still, when we scratched under the service, we identified that these recently developed services were often out of sync with their underpinning legacy services.

The client used multiple management frameworks and methodologies across its multiple towers and geographically dispersed departments as an organisation. However, these were often used seemingly in opposition to one another as opposed to adopting a blended approach. Additionally, many third-party suppliers were distanced from the organisational strategies and values, each operating their own framework interpretations; these were detached from the co-creation of value for their customers.

The net result was employees, customers and consumers expressing dissatisfaction with services not reflected in monthly service management and C-level reviews – an example of watermelon SLAs done 'to' the organisation.

For those of us who had worked in service management for some time, this was a familiar problem, one we'd sometimes been guilty of developing ourselves. This experience taught us to propose a blended approach to this issue.

Our proposal at that moment, and the feeling with all that has been learned before and since, is that IT service management should shift its focus to the organisation, delivering digital products and services that enabled the co-creation of value for service customers via a value-driven community – as opposed to just targeting IT strategy and delivery. We needed to align the organisational strategy with the digital and enterprise teams' value-based outcomes and objectives.

This began by engaging people from across the organisation and its suppliers to look at services more holistically, agreeing on a joint approach to co-create real value to digital services' continuous delivery and development. We took people out of their day-to-day work once a week via a value-focused CoP; building a service quality charter that was focused on value-based outcomes defining how we would co-create value and measured our steps to success, with the aim of scaling and lifting these throughout the organisation.

To achieve this, we knew we could not simply adopt a 'big bang' approach. We identified and engaged our sponsors, selecting just a few services and teams to focus on. We considered not only their role but also their influence, their input, and their impact on digital service definition, digital service production and digital service support, along with their formal and informal interaction with service customers.

We progressed iteratively with our stakeholders, continually seeking input and feedback; this led to us creating a sustainable value-focused CoP that could influence others. Our initial group was made up of global consumer-facing teams as well as those at the C-level, including champions at each level who would support a continual and iterative improvement ethos.

During these fact-finding sessions and later value-focused CoP meetings, we often found teams working in opposition to one another: differences in strategy, objectives or culture were obvious. Mostly this opposition occurred because the teams only worked 'together' during – or because of – stressful, urgent situations such as a major incident, a failed change or a time-critical presentation.

To counter this, we adopted an approach based on ALOE (asking, listening, observing, empathising), discovering that teams felt less restricted by working in a practice rather than 'within' a process. We used our service management experiences to highlight where we had seen similar issues before and used our knowledge to build a roadmap towards success based on value-focused outcomes.

Taking these teams out of 'the trenches' and into a safe environment immediately removed the stress of those situations. Each of the teams contributed to, and ultimately agreed on, a service quality charter that reflected the values of the organisation and the community, a team that grew as people sought to get involved over the weeks and months. Our value-focused CoP was born.

This community grew from a handful of members to become a global team of influencers and impactors, with a strong focus on service quality. From here, we were able to influence not only the value-focused outcomes of the community, but we were also able to create new roles and define objectives that were taken on by teams from across the enterprise.

Positive results came quickly with proof-of-concept services that the community agreed on. We grew our understanding of the services through value-based conversations, moving on to splitting out our teams to map the current and desired state for the services, both technical and non-technical, and resources, partners, measures and governance layers.

We also set out to understand whether the services were being received well by customers and consumers, leading us to look most closely at those watermelon services that were reporting 'green' on a month-by-month basis yet had less than positive customer or consumer feedback.

Not only did this CoP (and those that came after) embed continual improvement as a practice across digital services and their lifecycle, but we also identified role gaps across the organisation, set team objectives that became organisational objectives, and informed the organisation's technology roadmap and strategy (among many other positive outcomes).

Whether they worked in the people and culture, finance or digital teams, and whether they were a developer, supporter or consumer of the services, each member of the community played a part in both co-creating and implementing value into digital services, they did so in an iterative manner. Our feedback loops made everyone feel part of what became an ongoing success story. Over time, these communities grew as those within the enterprise saw positive outcomes. They were no longer IT-centric; the communities tackled enterprise issues on behalf of the whole organisation.

In one case, we began to see a logo we had developed for our CoP continually appear on presentations and on screens around the global headquarters of the customer. This was a great indicator that our chosen collaboration and communication methods were having a positive impact.

Figure 4: CoP Logo

CoPs have recently sprung up in industry discussion, reaching beyond traditional IT processes and practices. They are now influencing the enterprise as a whole, using all of the lessons learned in ITSM over the last 40 years – as well as picking up new ways of working from established problem-solving and innovation techniques used in other enterprise business areas.

Your CoP should aim to focus on the value it can add to your enterprise and the community therein; this should be shared appropriately. If you can, I would recommend that you record community meetings if using online video conferencing; I'd also recommend sharing agendas in a creative manner.

IBM Global Services taught me that an agenda is important; it helps community members prioritise, and intrigues existing and potential members. It's with this in mind that I include real examples of value-focused CoP agendas on the following pages.

Figure 5: CoP Agenda

Figure 6: CoP Agenda

Figure 7: CoP Agenda

Figure 8: CoP Agenda

Figure 9: CoP Agenda

Figure 10: CoP Agenda

Figure 11: CoP Agenda

Summary

Much ground has been covered in this chapter, and I'd hasten to add that a lot more ground needs to be covered by everyone who works in and around our industry and beyond.

One client I worked with had a great vision statement of 'Always Learning'. If you are reading this, I'm sure you are already thinking of different ways that enterprise-focused service management can enable your organisation; I'd hope you are critiquing what you've read and debating it with yourself. That is a great thing if we are all thinking about the how and the why.

In essence, this chapter and the enablement of organisations using value-focused CoPs to discuss and embed enterprise-focused service management returns us to that controlled experimentation statement and that childlike curiosity I mention elsewhere. Service management is both of these things, with our cumulative knowledge, expertise and ability to read between the lines thrown in. Service management does enable organisations by involving those within the sector and beyond.

As mentioned above, this use of value co-creation using CoPs is spreading. Industry leaders such as itSMF UK are using CoPs to promote new ways of working, and CoPs are also being used to mentor and develop people en masse as well as to tackle subjects that are critical to the work environment and the world as a whole. This is just the beginning, and it's my opinion that a great value-focused CoP can make a positive difference.

The Enterprise Digital Podcast

In January 2023, I was lucky enough to be invited to guest on the Enterprise Digital podcast (a great resource for enterprise service management knowledge).[10] It was here that something strikingly obvious was put to me when discussing enterprise service management and value co-creation – something I'd not even thought of myself until that point. When discussing how we co-create enterprise service management value, the hosts Barclay Rae and Ian Aitchison summed it up beautifully by saying:

"The community puts the 'Co' into co-creating value."

This is the beauty of enterprise-focused service management and value-focused CoPs. We can work across industries and use what we learn to work together to co-create value for organisations, their employees, their customers and consumers. Added to all of this, we can influence organisational strategies and assist organisations in pivoting when something bonkers happens in the world.

This is the power of community.

[10] *https://podcasts.apple.com/gb/podcast/enterprise-digital-podcast-episode-61-co-creating-value/id1632185587?i=1000593952559*.

CHAPTER 7: ISN'T SERVICE MANAGEMENT BORING?

In asking this question, it's obvious that I have a bias, but in truth, I can see why some people may think service management is boring. It is a difficult career choice to explain.

It's not like you can say "I'm a carpenter" or 'I'm a soccer player", or to return to the earlier conversation, "I'm a ceramicist". Each of these career choices is clear to someone who is not in that role. You can see the outcome of their work and imagine their day-to-day activities. Service management as a career is harder to explain, and this can lead to the perception that it's boring.

Hopefully, you'll be forming a better understanding of what service management 'is' and what it 'isn't. In this chapter, I'd like to cover some real-world scenarios and examples from my career and those of others so that you can answer the question for yourself.

Failing that, there are great example's of ITSM and the importance of 'people' in Table 4 that will help you answer the question in the future.

Lies, darn lies and statistics

In October 2022, I conducted a poll on LinkedIn titled:

Is service management boring?

This poll generated over 2100 engagements on LinkedIn and delivered the results in Figure 12.

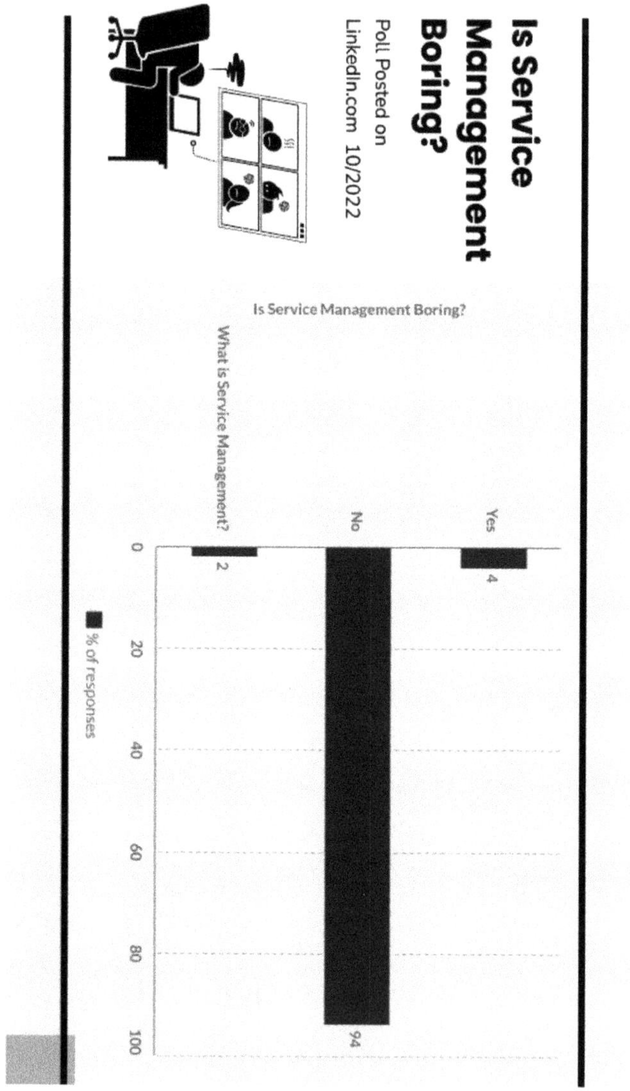

Figure 12: Is Service Management Boring? Poll Results From October 2022

Most responders (94%) voted that service management is not boring. Of these, the vast majority of responders were or had been working in ITSM, so also had an element of bias in their votes.

The comments associated with the poll were of equal interest, some of which I've highlighted and responded to below. I have chosen not to disclose the identity of the responders to protect their privacy. If you are reading this and commented, thank you ever so much for your input!

Table 4: LinkedIn Poll Respondent Comments and Author's Thoughts

Responder Comment	Author's Response
It's as boring as you make it...two people could deliver exactly the same initiatives, workshops etc...with completely different levels of engagement, excitement, adoption...it's all about the people.	*Each* of these comments is so true. Service management is a people business. People enable the technology as much as, if not more than, the technology enables people. These comments validate the reasons why people skills, communication and the building of communities are vital to the enterprise-wide success of service management as well as any other organisational improvement.
The *people are the most important Enablers as well as the biggest bottlenecks for any improvement to happen.* *Unfortunately! We the people are the very*	

Responder Comment	Author's Response
impediments to any of our own progress.	
Its only boring if it's just seen as processes and tools, and some sort of orthodoxy. *Whereas its actually about developing and improving people, business, management, and organisations. It's fun and rewarding to be a part of that and making change happen.*	
Boring means people judging inanimate things like processes and technology. When we consider the people aspect, it gives us purpose. For example, we care about incidents because people are impacted. Also, we care about Changes because they'll either fix someone's issue or give them new functionality. It's the purpose that matters.	Both comments relate to people and build upon this by discussing purpose. Another fantastic contribution. We often lose sight of those impacted and the value we can add to someone's day, let alone strategic and organisational value. When looking at the process or the implementation of new

Responder Comment	Author's Response
When you focussed on Purpose & Outcome, I definitely agree, it is so important to know these two aspects to say the least. *I have seen people getting transformed from "Boring" to "Intelligent enough" when they really understood the Purpose and intended Outcome.*	technology, it really does pay to consider it from the perspective of those you hope will benefit from the initiative. If you know what you are doing on a process from the outside in, it is likely you'll reduce waste by cutting out an unnecessary step, i.e., those steps that don't add any value to the person using the process or those steps that are not required from an organisational or regulatory perspective. With technology initiatives, it's no different. Looking at your new shiny thing through the lens of its consumer or user may well provide a view point you hadn't considered and enable you to add value through an additional output or indeed an improvement in value through reducing functionality – more isn't always better.

Responder Comment	Author's Response
	We then return to people. Co-create this value through conversation and ALOE.
Anything that is not understood by People will be perceived as "Boring" by a majority of people. The remaining few will still be inquisitive to know cos they have a "thirst for gaining knowledge about the unknown". *Even if people know the importance of something (Framework, Methodology, Standard etc...) but if they don't get to lay their hands on it and Practice it and realise the benefits, then soon they will lose interest if not feel boring.* *If any Service is not managed holistically in all its dimensions, very soon the Service will lose Value and will reach end of life. Therefore Service Management should be a mandatory inclusion in*	This comment touches on everything above and adds a layer I feel passionately about. Education. It's the reason I wanted to put this book together, to educate us all on the benefits of service management – to those seeking to make a career, those seeking to progress and to those leaders trying to understand who and how to enable those people to deliver successful ITSM outcomes to their enterprise organisations. I'm aware of young people taking further education in computer science who have no idea that service management exists, let alone what it is.

Responder Comment	Author's Response
College as well as University courses. The more awareness the more will be the adoption and adaptation of Service Management Principles & Practices along with Governance.	Many of those I know who work in the industry fell into it. We've discussed the common consensus that the IT industry per se has existed for give or take 80 years. In the last 40 years and certainly since the advent of the Internet approximately 30 years ago, IT has woven itself into the fabric of everyday life and business. We now have a generational group of experts working in the industry, who have picked up these learnings through applying service management across different industries. This is something this industry didn't have before as it was too young. Added to this we have new generations, ideas and beliefs coming into the industry – a generation that has grown up with digital

Responder Comment	Author's Response
	services, who see the need to put digital at the heart of everything we do. But these people are not merely limited to working in enterprise service management or even IT. They are found throughout organisations and realise the benefit of digital enablement as part of their everyday lives. I believe we are working at the perfect time to achieve that consistent approach. Anything we can do to influence education, whether formally via educational establishments or via professional bodies, is incredibly important in developing the industry and those within it, those planning to get involved and even those who have no idea it exists.
But people who drone on endlessly about the semantics are. I had a discussion yesterday about	This comment is so reflective of everyday life in service management – in

Responder Comment	Author's Response
whether recurring Incidents should be attached to a 'Master' Incident that is left open for that purpose, or to a Problem. It doesn't matter was my conclusion. Provided you know that's how you work. *Now I am bored!!*	organisations that implement it by the book. On the one hand, it's vital to have a common understanding of 'language', but this should really be a basic thing that's bottomed out as a process is implemented or developed. The contributor is so correct, in that it really doesn't matter as long as you know that's how you work – and that 'it' works. Service management is not rocket science; if it was, many of us would be doing something else.
Your answer is going to be biased. We should ask CIOs and other non-ITSM professionals if they think Service Management is boring. Although back to the question, I agree it is not boring for many of the reasons my colleagues have stated.	A perfect response, and one that really highlights the need to think and work holistically as well as to gather feedback iteratively. Implementing a feedback loop across your organisation is vital. Doing so via an all-encompassing community is perfect. Both

Responder Comment	Author's Response
	take work and both will ultimately need an element of team empowerment and time from the CIO and other non-ITSM professionals.
It is a big part of my professional existence and I do only things that really excite me, so the answer is NO! But theory can be boring and the ton of books and material we need to swallow is quite boring though it helps you fall asleep at night. *I still love the step I took in 1999 to dive into this and I am pretty sure I will retire with it. Not by being certified like a war hero, but by being a true practitioner of Service Management in all its facets and potential.* *Next to my wife this is the love of my life!*	Next to my wife, this is the love of my life. Wow! Here we have a passionate contributor who writes wise words (though I wonder what their significant other(s) think). It's all true – it's not the certifications that make us. They help with baselining our understanding, they help us to get our foot in the door – but it's how we deliver as practitioners that helps us co-create and deliver value-based outcomes. I'm sorry to add to the ton of books – I hope this one proves useful.

Responder Comment	Author's Response
I like to compare Service Management with organisations like an airport, the value streams, the airplane, and the service managers putting in place all the essentials like boarding desks, customs, security, shops, fuelling, baggage handling, air traffic control, etc. Or working on the bridge of a huge cruise ship. Perhaps our environments are not as sexy but the work, putting the right building blocks in place is as rewarding.	I adore this comment. Why? Service management is all of these things. When the plane takes off, it's IT systems will have been through service design and continually improved with a value-focused outcome to ensure and improve passenger safety (an airline's number one priority). Along with the that, ITSM will run customs services, deliver a process to ensure baggage handling is automated and potentially have seen a major incident when the passport scanners failed last night, with an emergency change implemented to get passengers moving. These aspects are service management in a nutshell.
Anything that gives you insights on how you're doing and can do better can never be boring.	Yes, yes, yes. That's what we do, and now we can do it in real-time and predict the future (really, we can). This is an epic part of service management and is

Responder Comment	Author's Response
	as far from boring as I can imagine.
Information Technology Service Management isn't boring, but frameworks usually are.	Ever so true. As is the endless 'which framework' debate. I suggest using the frameworks to inform your ways of working but do not adopt them by the book. Like a cook, take the recipe, adapt it, and blend the ingredients to work for you and your consumers.
Hahaha makes me laugh. *Like you read my mind.* *Like anything there is really boring stuff, and usually it's the admin stuff.* *Agile and Product Management also has boring stuff that has to be done.* *But there's also interesting stuff like mapping out a broken incident process*	If I make someone laugh, it makes my day – as long as they are not laughing at me. These comments are reflective of most practices and workplaces. I expect none of us really want to work and certainly not on something boring. ITSM enables people to work in any industry. This, for me, makes it exciting and over time you can pick and choose where you work to follow a passion project – hence my time working in

Responder Comment	Author's Response
and fixing it, figuring out to eliminate non-value add stuff, automating repetitive work, or designing an integrated IT-business service…loads more in the 'interesting' column than the 'boring' column I think.	education and my desire to work in sustainable energy. Though if any jobs come up with Liverpool FC, I'd be over the moon.
I love working in Service Management. I get to be involved in things across the technology function as well as across the business. It's awesome, fun and I get to work with all sorts of different people too.	A great comment to finish on. It's the perfect summary of why service management is not boring.

"I don't need service management"

At the risk of repeating myself, I want to address a statement that has been presented to me several times over the years. The statement is incredibly relevant, and how you respond to it as an ITSM professional can make or break any number of scenarios, not least your career.

For example, during a meeting in 2022, I was greeted with the following, delivered with a wry smile:

"We don't need service management; in fact, we are pretty pleased with how we chew up IT service managers and spit them out."

I've heard some considered statements before, but none that went so far as to chew up and spit out service managers. That said, it's an interesting comment and one that I didn't see echoed by the team of people receiving the digital service my client was providing. I saw a team of people who, though not audibly supportive of the statement, were incredibly interested to see how this self-proclaimed ITSM expert would respond. My response was simple:

"Tell me why you don't need service management."

It was from this point that the conversation both with the person making the statement and their team developed. It was not my intention to convince them; I truly wanted to understand why.

We began by discussing their desired outcomes in delivering service to their customers. This particular business unit serviced customers via the telephone, so we started from this point. We discussed everything that was going well, but it was only a short time until we touched upon the challenges involved in delivering a great set of service outcomes.

Once I had understood these challenges and the desired outcomes, I could use my experiences working on helpdesks to empathise.

We discussed how we could enable them to manage and deliver high-quality call centre services to their customers and one another through consolidating knowledge.

As a team, I noticed that people had different roles, and I asked how they shared knowledge. They said there were occasions when knowledge handover was complex as people were constantly on calls. I made a few minor suggestions on how these gaps could be closed, leading to improved knowledge sharing.

We then talked about new starters; as a call centre, staff requirements could be seasonal with peaks and troughs. In their case, onboarding new team members was a complicated process that needed to be more expedient in its nature. Through conversation, I was able to ask if there were any pre-defined periods where they would expect a peak – and there were.

From this point, we could map out these dates and the expected numbers within a 20% tolerance. We also discussed those elements that needed more expediency and reduced difficulty. As a team, we took these away and removed any unnecessary steps from the process. We also began to integrate anticipation and automation for the new-starter process; these were designed to improve both the speed of onboarding and the ease for the call centre team.

Importantly, we were able to have a conversation where we gathered more of an idea of one another's responsibilities within this global organisation. Doing so enabled these business owners, me, and all of those on the call to better understand the internal needs of this vital business function and our roles in delivering these service outcomes.

Our meeting was only 90 minutes, so it took a lot of work to change the mindset completely, but what we did was show the benefit of service management and its key skills of ALOE (asking, listening, observing and empathising). It had turned out that the application and delivery of service management had mainly been based on things the business unit wasn't interested in – such as watermelon SLAs, historical reporting, and a lack of empathy for their ongoing business issues, which had led to this team just taking the work and placing the management of risk onto themselves. They didn't need someone to tell them what they already knew.

Another powerful aspect of this conversation is that we managed to get these stakeholders on board. Those who had remained silent were now contributing ideas to work together. Even though they were a harder nut to crack, our key stakeholders had softened and have since received some ITSM-related improvements. These improvements have been introduced into the business, following a set of co-created and predefined goals that would illustrate success or otherwise.

Through tracking and ensuring that these goals are met, we were able to improve iteratively and continually break down the challenges and turn them into a more successful practice.

Another key aspect is that I have never asked if the 'need' for service management has changed. Truthfully, I have never heard 'I need service management', but I have heard 'thank you for the improvements'.

I'll take that.

Summary

As we conclude this chapter, I'd like to think that you, as a reader, understand why I and others believe service management is not boring. Running my poll and seeing an engagement of 2100 people on LinkedIn illustrates an 'interest' in service management that even I was previously unaware of; it was a pleasant surprise.

The comments in this chapter and those elsewhere regarding the value of service management and the type of professionals suited to service management illustrate that it is not boring to those involved. However, it can still be perceived as such by those who are not working in or around it as an organisational enabler.

Through writing this book, I'm keen to address the 'understanding' issue and the 'boring' question. Still, I won't pretend that this will change much, as it is unlikely that you'll be reading this passage unless you have at least a passing interest in the profession.

That's where you as a reader come in; we need to work together as service management professionals and continually illustrate our value through delivering what we learn when strategising, designing, transitioning, operating and improving digital IT services into enterprise ecosystems.

We need to communicate our successes appropriately. One way to do so is to share our service management stories with our community of colleagues, customers, consumers, partners and leaders.

We can ask that they listen as we explain the value we offer; we can demonstrate this through measurement and observation of our organisational successes and build empathy for the challenges we face. We can use ALOE to build an understanding that service management isn't boring – it's all around them.

Or we can share how service management saved the lives of an elephant and a diver.

CHAPTER 8: WHY SERVICE MANAGEMENT ISN'T BORING – TALES FROM THE AUTHOR

As we begin this chapter, we see how changing the words in a sentence into a different order can materially change the point. Our last chapter, titled "Isn't Service Management Boring?", becomes "Why Service Management Isn't Boring".

Truthfully, service management is just like anything; sometimes it's boring and other times it's super exciting.

Service management as a profession is like any other; there are days where you grind and wonder, 'What did I achieve today?' and there are other days where it feels like the world is moving so fast that you are just willing it to slow down.

Working in ITSM for over 30 years has thrown up some interesting, weird and wonderful situations. Some of these can be shared, and others must forever remain secrets due to client or even government confidentiality and security; these alone make this profession anything but boring.

As a service management professional, you can work strategically in the boardroom of worldwide brands or at the heart of government or in investment banking on a trading floor. You are usually at the bleeding edge of technology and innovation.

You may also spend your days in these environments tactically resolving major IT incidents that can cost billions of pounds, ruin an organisation's reputation and threaten its very existence or indeed endanger human life. I've worked in all three scenarios and many more. These have been some of the most extreme moments of my entire life, in or out of work. And while the adrenaline rush was almost addictive, these events had a national or international significance. Over time, these taught me so many lessons both in and out of my professional existence.

The tales I'll share are two of the more 'fun' tales I am able to share.

These true stories are from the early 2000s as I figure I won't get into trouble, and technology has moved on a little since these times.

In fact, technology and working practices are driven to continually improve as a result of similar scenarios, where service management professionals need to implement and design solutions to these incidents. Our world in the early 2000s was similar, but our redundancy and design were behind where they're at today.

How service management saved an elephant's life

I'm a Service Management professional, not a storyteller, and my memory is not what it was. However, one thing I've always done is to keep my notes from every role, and this is why these two stories of Service Management tales of old are somewhat shareable.

We live in a world connected to the World Wide Web 24 hours a day, and this was no different back in the early 2000s. This meant my job for a worldwide finance brand was a 24/7/365 role. I was the ITSM world's equivalent to a fireman – a major incident manager.

No two days were the same, and frequently, you'd be about to leave work for home or do something for fun when the phone rang, and you'd need to spring into life.

There I was fast asleep in my flat in Brighton, UK, at around 2 am when that familiar rumble of my pager (yes, it was that long ago) informed me that my client's Internet connection was down at their Indian office with intermittent outages across other sites globally.

In this situation, I wore a few different hats – facilitator, communicator and technical manager, with my objectives being to:

- Ensure all technical teams were engaged in a major incident conference bridge;
- Ensure everyone on the 'need to know' list was told what was going on via email, pager and telephone; and
- Restore the Internet service to the client!

I didn't welcome this level of responsibility at 2 am, but I was used to it, so we brought the correct technical people to the 'bridge'. We initialised communications to our global stakeholders and set to work on identifying the cause of the Internet outage.

Before we go into what we found and what we did, I'd like to explain the impact of this major incident 'Internet' outage. Our client could not effectively trade with its customers and consumers; colleagues were working from paper as opposed to IT, and the world was not going to stop spinning fast.

We began by looking at the things we 'owned'.

Was everything in the impacted sites powered on? Were there any errors flashing up that could establish the cause? Had we done anything ourselves via the change management process to cause the outage? In each of these cases, there was no identifiable cause.

We extended our search and reached out to our suppliers, where our first indicator of cause became known. We were not the only organisation impacted by this issue. In fact, our Internet supplier could tell us each organisation or district impacted as they had a fault on one of their 'lines' – the cables that delivered communications and Internet to us and to other organisations in the region.

At this point, some customers began to reconnect to the Internet. 'Hurrah', we sang – before they reported it down again, while others said they could work.

It turned out that we were not looking at a fault on just one line – or one cable. It was impacting multiple cables. Each of these was designed to offer redundancy and connect Internet services across India and the world.

Time for a brief history lesson (which I didn't have at the time).

Cabling for the Internet is pre-dated by approximately 150 years when the telegraph network was implemented. At the end of the 20th century, there was a mixture of these old cables and recently installed fibre optic cables deployed all over the world via land, sea and, at this point, in just a few cases, from space. Connecting distant continents, some of this cabling is older and more fallible than others.

In the case of our client and the Internet consumers impacted by this intermittent series of outages, our investigations discovered that their connections depended on thousands of kilometres of undersea cables that criss-cross the oceans of the entire planet.

We were edging closer to our cause; in this case, it was an undersea earthquake.

Initial root-cause investigation suggested our connection failures were caused by an undersea earthquake breaking the Internet connection into India coming in from the African continent; this, in turn, meant that connections into Mumbai from the ocean were suffering intermittent failures.

Yet here is the odd thing: our land-based connection was showing more uptime than those coming in via the ocean floor – it was somehow similarly impacting customers but with less impact on their operations' work.

In this case, our organisation had stood up our major incident communications bridge. We'd engaged the Internet service provider, and as a result, there seemed little point in organisations A, B and C having three more bridge calls, so they joined ours. I was now, in effect, the major incident manager for billions of pounds worth of companies and their assets in a scenario where an undersea earthquake had seemingly brought us all to a halt – and I was doing this on two hours' sleep from a flat in Brighton. It was now dawn for me, and rather ironically, I had a great view of the sun rising over the ocean.

While I was sat in my flat wondering what was going to happen next and who else I had to tell, my colleagues and customers in India were well into their business day with limited Internet traffic, and our engineers were on the call continuing to troubleshoot how they would get things working. We even had a chap from the Internet provider sitting in Texas, where you could hear the sound of crickets in the background while Joe (name changed) gently chewed tobacco. This was a truly global effort.

Our teams' investigations kept pointing to an intermittent fault above ground in India itself, which was seemingly running between a couple of hubs that the client organisation and our engineers could deduce was within a 30 km radius of one of the sites.

Note: The life of a service management professional is curious from the perspective that I know that engineers can do these great techy things. Such as discovering where an Internet connection is dropping – though I still have minimal idea how. I believe it's something to do with sending a signal until a break is detected, with the time the signal travels before breaking equating to the distance around which the break is likely to be.

What we found when they located the precise location of the issue was something else entirely; we found an elephant on the floor – actually, it was in a ditch and wrapped around its legs (which it had pinned under itself) was a cable. You've guessed it, this was our Internet cable, and it was damaged as a result of this incident.

Now don't quote me on this, but there is a belief that wild and domestic animals possess a sixth sense – and know in advance when the earth will shake. I cannot be sure if this elephant was knocked down by the undersea earthquake, but in a twist of fate, something had shocked the elephant into collapsing into a ditch.

So here we were, intermittent Internet connections, an undersea earthquake, and a collapsed elephant seemingly stopping half of the world's finance businesses from operating. I'd had more straightforward Thursday nights and Friday mornings. Nobody was dragging me away from this one!

Our poor elephant had broken its leg, so we could not simply repair the cable as before we could do anything, we had to make the elephant comfortable and remove it safely for its own health. When I asked how long that could take on the bridge call, I was told it could be days or even weeks! In this case, the elephant needed veterinary help. In a stroke of luck, an on-call vet was contacted, and they were within an hour of travel to the unfortunate animal.

Next up was coordinating rescue efforts for the elephant once it was made comfortable by the vet; this is where having feet on the ground reporting back to the major incident communications bridge was so good. Our local teams found a farmer with a tractor and a winch, who had seen this situation before. By the end of the day in India, the farmer was working with the vet and winching the elephant to a safe place for treatment and rehabilitation.

Service management had saved the elephant's life!

I appreciate that this is not quite true, but a little artistic licence is good for the book and had we not been looking for an Internet issue, we may have never been in a position to help the elephant.

Once the elephant was safely dispatched, our team identified that the cable in question had been laid on the floor (or had come to lay on the floor) and had indeed been dragged and broken by the elephant. This, in turn, had left enough connectivity for just a little connection but not enough for our sites to be connected. Once understood, the team set about repairing the cable, and we saw site-to-site connectivity fully restored BUT not full Internet access.

Unfortunately, we hadn't fully restored service, and it was now well into Friday evening in the UK – but at least we had the weekend to get things up and running; surely, that would be enough time…

How service management saved a deep-sea diver's life

With our intermittent Internet outage now moving towards 24 hours, we were still working as a global team on our major incident conference bridge, trying to circumvent the Internet issue while attempting to locate our broken cabling on the seabed.

Nowadays, even though these cables use more modern technology and are more resistant, they do occasionally break or suffer damage for a number of reasons, including fishing, anchoring and, in this case in the early 2000s, the undersea earthquake.

Our conversations on the bridge call included whether there had been another cause of cable breakage. Although we did not feel it was the case in our situation, it was a topic that would come home to roost.

The people sent out to find the break and repair the seabed cable mentioned that it wasn't just undersea earthquakes or even ships anchoring that can cause cable breakages – something else had seemingly been the cause on other occasions – sharks!

As the call went on, we were also becoming acutely aware of the cost and time involved in repairing undersea cables.

When they broke, a telecommunications operator had to find the location of the failure point, bring the damaged part to the surface, and replace it with a new length of cable.

Once we had located a break, our team were dispatched to the site to repair it; luckily, there were only a few hours away. It was at the point of bringing the cable to the surface that we began to become aware of a couple of issues:

- Retrieving the cable from the seabed was proving more difficult for the crew tasked with doing so. A combination of debris within the sea and persistent machinery issues meant that some of the work had to be manually undertaken by divers.
- While preparing to enter the water to undertake this work, our divers became aware of another interested party. That of sharks.

All of this was being reported back to me on dry land in the UK. I'm unaware of any manual for such a situation, so I was lucky that some people on the major incident bridge had seen this before! Another element that was quite 'fun' in this scenario was my responsibility to communicate the ongoing status to our stakeholders. Among them were some rather senior business leaders, so they must have been as perplexed as I was amused when my status updates read the lines below.

Latest update: Connection partially restored as an elephant has been lifted from the impacted cable by a local farmer.

Or

Latest update: Currently finding out how to remove sharks from the area of the current undersea investigations.

I had interacted mostly via speakerphone and mostly at home, so my wife was privy to all of this and wondered what on earth was going on.

The people that had seen this scenario before, as well as those at sea, agreed that it may be wise to radio out to see if any vessels nearby were prepared to head their way and entice the shark with food, allowing the divers to retrieve the cable and make the necessary repairs.

This was not like summoning a takeaway: many calls were made, and many options were discussed, but over the course of the next 18 hours or so, progress was made, and the cable was repaired.

In this case, service management saved a diver's life!

Once again, I appreciate that this is not quite true and that, once more, a little artistic licence is good for the book. However, our ITSM practice of having a centralised major incident communications bridge had brought all the necessary parties together to constructively discuss approaching this bizarre situation.

It had also returned services to not just one organisation but to multiple organisations.

ITSM practices provided an element of order that meant we could agree on a stepped approach to the situation and remove any panic in restoring the services. We were also able to articulate clearly, communicate all the necessary information to our stakeholders, and implement workarounds where possible. All of this bought us time, which meant we could take a considered approach to the elephant and the divers' predicaments and manage those situations appropriately.

Had service management not been present in this situation, it could have taken longer to resolve the incident, and stakeholders would not have had much idea of what was going on over the course of a few days. ITSM provided order and communication despite the madness of the situation. It also provided a joined-up approach to capture the lessons learned and to suggest improvements to prevent or mitigate future similar scenarios.

Root cause, permanent resolution and improvement?

I'd been involved in many major IT incidents up to this point. Still, I hadn't been involved in one that spanned continents, nor one that impacted so many customers and consumers of those Internet-based services.

Until this point, I'd had no desire or inclination to consider that there was a global network of underwater cables that form a large part of the Internet's backbone. During this incident and our follow-up discussion, I realised that these cables carry the majority of data around the world and eventually link up to the networks that deliver Internet services to continents and countries; there is a subsea of cables that connect New York to London and Australia to Los Angeles.

Added to this, there are areas of the ocean where there is so much movement of goods, people, etc. that there are literal points of the ocean where these cables exist and have a much greater potential to break and disrupt global Internet connection. Known in the trade as points of failure.

Subsea cables are relatively fragile and easily damaged. Every year, even today, there are more than 100 incidents where the cables are cut or damaged. The majority of these are caused by shipping or environmental damage.

Back in the early noughties, there was less resilience in these areas than there is today, and this is where service management at least contributed to what we see today in terms of resilience and improved uptime.

Our root cause was relatively straightforward to come up with – an undersea earthquake and, to some extent, a stranded elephant.

More interesting and difficult was the permanent resolution. In this case, we had to bite off what we could chew (pun intended), which was to make recommendations based on this incident, its impact and the cost to the organisations impacted versus the cost of reducing the chances of this reoccurring. Sadly ITSM cannot prevent undersea earthquakes. Also, we do not control the purse strings for organisations. (Though it's my opinion that we should be involved in those conversations as a digital IT strategy is key to enabling an organisation's business goals).

There are, however, things ITSM, along with ongoing investment and innovation, can do. It can suggest areas of resilience, discuss innovative techniques to improve awareness of potential earthquakes and implement process improvements should these things reoccur in the future.

In the immediate aftermath, we focused on what we could do, and much of this came down to the notes I'd taken. I keep a lot of notes, and this book owes itself to them. In this case, they were a great way of playing back what had happened, which enabled us to use knowledge management to clean up my notes and use them in the future if such an incident were to reoccur – and it did.

In this second major incident, there were no elephants or sharks. Still, we were able to step through our investigations from the previous incident to take proactive steps we'd been unable to take before, which substantially reduced the period where any Internet impact was felt. We improved communications by contacting the right people at the right time, which our customers were pleased about.

As is clear from this major incident, we were not the only organisation impacted by this or similar Internet outages that were caused by cable breakage. In every case, ITSM teams (whether labelled as this or not) would have conducted similar root-cause and permanent resolution investigations via the likes of knowledge management and problem management, adding those they couldn't immediately resolve to a risk register or a continual-improvement initiative.

As each organisation conducted these exercises, they were building up a series of risk-based investment and business cases that would go on to justify the time and investment needed to add further resilience and standards to running the Internet through cables. Even down to simple things like the land-based service provider carrying out 'eyeball' checks on the cabling in India to ensure it was run in a safe place (i.e., not dragged across the floor) in these pre-fibre cable times.

Since our major incident, and as a result of other major incidents and those lessons learned, there has been far more resilience added to the Internet. It is no longer quite so easy to take down large parts of it and suffocate trade or consumer activities.

Nowadays, companies that send data through subsea Internet cables don't just use one cable but will have space on multiple cables. If one cable fails, traffic is eventually rerouted through others, which means that the consumer of those Internet services will notice little to no impact even though the service provider will probably have people like me on calls at 2 am to repair elements of the services to ensure the resilience remains in place.

Unfortunately, this is not the same everywhere; there still exist some areas where the impact can be great. One example is Tonga, where there is only one cable, and therefore breakages can have devastating impacts. In addition, those lessons learned from us have illustrated a real need for redundancy.

This is why Google, Facebook and Microsoft have spent hundreds of millions of dollars on their subsea Internet cables in recent years.

In recent years, we have seen a greater prevalence of satellite Internet, as recently popularised by Elon Musk's Starlink project. This kind of system doesn't offer a replacement for underwater cables. Satellites are used for providing connectivity in rural locations or as emergency backups. Still, they can't replace physical infrastructure entirely as they cannot carry data across continents as easily as cables. This is a great step in the right direction as more and more of the world gets connected.

Summary

Service management is not boring! It's full of different roles and scenarios, and enables you to work anywhere in the world in any industry.

Suppose you apply service management from an enterprise perspective. In that case, you can get involved in managing multi-billion-pound technology services, building digital careers frameworks that provide an opportunity to colleagues and deliver innovation globally. You can speak at events, write blogs and podcast about it.

If you focus purely on the IT elements, you can contribute towards improving the world's connectivity and even saving the lives of elephants and divers.

Repeat after me; service management is not boring! ☺

CHAPTER 9: WHAT MAKES A GREAT SERVICE MANAGEMENT PROFESSIONAL?

I hope by now you'll have recognised yourself or your team members as the 'type' of people who may perform well as service management professionals.

This role is fairly new; some people fall into it and have no idea how they got there. It's a role that can 'creep' up on you, and before you know it, you are on a call at 2 am investigating an Internet outage, or you are managing a multibillion-pound digital service that will make the international news if it falls over.

It would please me so much if this profession could become a more defined career path; therefore, in this chapter, we'll cover those elements that make a great service management professional. We'll also cover useful certifications that you could use to stimulate yourself and your career in this profession.

Service management has a number of roles that exist to deliver IT services. I have covered many of these roles, so I believe I can offer a unique insight into what makes a great service management professional.

My roles have included the following:

- Service desk analyst.
- Service desk leader.
- Problem manager.
- Customer satisfaction and continual improvement leader.
- Major incident manager.

- Service management process writer.
- Change manager.
- Knowledge manager.
- Problem, incident, major incident and change leader.
- Service transition leader.
- Service designer.
- Head of service management.
- Service management consultant.
- Independent service management consultant.
- Enterprise service management consultant.

Although it may appear that way, this exercise was not a self-indulgent promotion of myself; it was designed to illustrate my journey so far and the type of journey you, as a prospective or current service management professional, may be able to take.

I am NOT an expert in all things service management; simply put, technology and our volatile, uncertain, complex, ambiguous (VUCA) world is changing at a pace that makes it hard to keep up. Not to mention that 'how' you apply service management has a strong dependency on the environment in which you are applying it.

So, to give you a more rounded view, I have invited several of my trusted connections to provide their thoughts on this question from their perspectives; all I asked was for them to respond to the title of this chapter:

What makes a great service management professional?

From here, I will independently add my own view so I may round up the views of my connections.

From a Recruiter's Perspective

Alex Conroy
Senior Practice Manager, Reed

"As an IT recruiter, I cover Service Management requirements for clients across the public and private sectors. The job seekers I meet include service desk analysts, problem and change managers, service designers and heads of Service Management.

The end goal is the same in all these roles: to deliver a valued service for customers.

As recruitment consultants, we become skilled at recognising the qualities that make someone a great fit for a role – it's not only what's on a CV that matters. The candidates that stand out for us have more than good technical knowledge. They demonstrate soft skills like building a rapport with people and being calm and patient under pressure. They are confident enough to communicate effectively at all levels to get the job done and are unafraid to take on less glamorous tasks when necessary. Interpersonal skills are vital to get the best from teams and keeping customers happy.

On any given day of any digital service, a variety of challenges can arise that will test character more than anything else. Those who are resilient, adaptable and enjoy problem-solving are born to Service Management – and many organisations struggling to fill these types of vacancies externally will likely find they already employ people who would excel at the task if given the chance and upskilled.

We know it can be difficult for job seekers to market themselves beyond their CV and convince employers they would be a great fit. That's why recruiters can be so valuable in giving professionals a chance to present their true selves in our preliminary meetings with them. We can identify their motivations and ambitions and draw out what makes them ideal for a service role, whether it's a positive attitude, leadership qualities, or tenacity. These are the things of real value to employers."

From a Service Management Manager's Perspective

Tracy Venter
Global Head of Service Management

"Having worked as a service management professional for many years, the most successful colleagues I have worked with display several common personality traits. Skills can be taught if you have a good base upon which to develop those skills.

Understanding that we are human and have varying personality traits and how to adapt one's behaviour to communicate effectively is a must. The ability to build rapport easily while displaying sincerity is an excellent place to start.

Taking responsibility for the services delivered to the customer, and caring about how services are delivered, ensures that the customer is assured you are in their corner, within reason, of course, which leads me onto the balance. Having a balanced view of the customer, business goals and longer-term strategies sets the tone for informed decisions.

Taking the time to understand the customer also allows for pre-emptive action. I've always believed that the service management professional is the lynchpin between sales and customer retention. Building trust with the customer allows the service management professional to have an influence on the best solution or service for a customer, not the one that attracts the most commission.

Supporting the operational teams is crucial. Having a level of empathy for the challenges the support team face will absolutely help drive improvement and promotes inclusion. Bringing the team into the improvement conversations is highly beneficial. Having a flexible approach is a great way to achieve the best outcome, in that all options are considered.

Tenacity plays a huge part in terms of success. Service is not an easy road to tread. However, there is nothing better than seeing one's hard work and determination come to the fore in the successful delivery of services!"

From a Service Management Manager's Perspective

Sundeep Singh
Service Strategy Lead

"To be a good service management professional for me starts with a strong set of personable skills that allow you to connect well to the challenges people face. Showing you can develop collaborative relationships, empathise and be a good listener cannot be understated to help positively support others. Great service management is all about how we enable business outcomes to be delivered, so possessing a service and customer-focused mindset is key.

You could be expected to cooperate with stakeholders across all levels, from customers to leaders in an organisation. Therefore, having the ability to communicate well, influence decisions and manage your time is important. You need not be a subject matter expert but having a broad awareness of the technology in your space and how to navigate new and emerging practices such as Cloud, Agile and DevOps in your toolkit can be a real benefit, especially if asked to translate technical dialogue into language that everyone understands.

Having an adaptable, can-do attitude will serve well when dealing with ambiguous situations. There's never any shortage of problem-solving to do in service management, so being analytical, creative, open-minded and curious to ask tough questions will be invaluable. Taking ownership and initiative, an interest in the bigger picture, showing proactiveness and striving with a desire for wanting to improve things are other important attributes I'd look for in a modern service management professional."

From a Service Management Manager's Perspective

Doug Oram
IT Service Management Leader

"A good service management professional should have a combination of personal attributes, core skills and behaviours that enable them to manage and deliver high-quality services and value to customers effectively.

Here are some of the key qualities to look for:

1. ***Customer-focused:*** *A service management professional should always be focused on meeting and exceeding customer expectations. They should understand the needs and concerns of their customers and be able to build and grow strong relationships with them.*

2. ***Communication skills:*** *Solid communication skills are critical as they must effectively communicate with customers (at all levels), stakeholders and team members, including written and verbal communication.*
3. ***Attention to detail:*** *Service management professionals should be detail-oriented, with a constant focus on quality and accuracy, even when managing multiple priorities and tasks.*
4. ***Analytical skills:*** *Service management professionals should be able to analyse support-related data and information to identify trends, patterns and potential areas of improvement. They should be able to use this information to make informed decisions and take action to improve the services they manage.*
5. ***Problem-solving skills:*** *Service management professionals should be able to assess problems as they arise; they should be able to work with the support team(s) and stakeholders to find solutions and implement improvements, thus preventing future issues and maintaining service stability.*
6. ***Flexibility:*** *The IT industry and technology landscape is constantly changing, so a good service management professional should be able to adapt to new technologies, processes and trends. They should be flexible and able to adjust their approach as needed to meet changing business requirements.*

Overall, a good service management professional should encompass all the above qualities, among others, such as patience, positivity and maintaining a sense of well-being.

9: What makes a great service management professional?

Service management can be quite stressful at times, so it is essential always to keep a level head, react positively (especially when dealing with customers), and always focus on a good work-life balance."

From a Service Management Educator's Perspective

Suzanne D. Van Hove, Ed.D.
CEO/Founder, SED-IT

"This is a question of characteristics, of which the following are my top five:

- ***Curiosity** – Can you think differently, push the edge of the envelope, and continually learn?*
- ***Critical thinking** – Can you assess without bias or predetermination? Can you apply the theoretical to the practical?*
- ***Business acumen** – What is the business, the goals/objectives, who are the customers, and what are their needs? What is the future?*
- ***Leadership** – Encourage autonomy and transparency, fail fast... Learn from each attempt, find the quick wins, mentor, ask the question, "How can I help?" If something isn't working or providing value, stop doing it. Just because we always have, doesn't mean we always should...*
- ***Organisation** – Juggling the ocean is never easy – the ability to prioritise based on need and benefit; keep a 'visual' plan in mind – what are the steps/stages, where are we, what is next – all with the ability to pivot as the*

environment and circumstances dictate – and still be able to meet the needs."

From a Service Management Educator's Perspective

Suzanne Galletly
Portfolio Director at EXIN

"Earlier, I discussed the 'new world' of service management. So, what does a 'good' service management professional look like in this new world view?

Well, understanding the basic principles behind service management is still crucial, although the changed context means that an integrated view of service management, such as that provided by SIAM and enterprise service management, is increasingly relevant. These approaches recognise that organisations are complex adaptive systems where the whole is greater than the sum of the parts – if integrated effectively. However, the service management professional of today needs much more than just knowledge of service management. A process-oriented way of working is extremely valuable, but an agile mindset is also needed to be able to continually adapt to changed circumstances, and lean thinking is important to understand value from the perspective of the customer.

But perhaps most important of all, we have the inherently 'human' competences and attributes that are required by service management professionals. These are the aspects that cannot be automated or taken over by artificial intelligence – at least, not yet.

These are:

- *Leadership, which is especially important if service management is to act as an enabler of transformation;*

- *Creativity to ensure services are continually improved and innovated;*
- *Judgement, so that decisions impacting service delivery are sound; and*
- *Empathy, to enable relationship building with all stakeholders involved in the service delivery.*

Finally, the only certainty we have in these fast-moving changes is that the next change is only around the corner, and this means that service management professionals need to adopt a lifelong-learning mindset so they can continually adapt their own behaviour and learn new skills. The learning never stops!"

From a Service Management Practitioner's Perspective

Matt Robinson (he/him)
IT Service Operations Manager

"I think good service management is a commitment to quality in the face of adversity. A drive to want to deliver value-add results despite the existing process, the poor documentation, the tooling limitations, and so on.

Good service management professionals are holistic, big-picture thinkers and consider collaboration and synergy to be tantamount. They value data and the importance of taking decisions based on evidence. They also know that decisions should be reached after results are analysed rather than seeking evidence to support conclusions.

I think service management professionals also understand the human element of the process, recognising that you have to ensure that processes are human-centric, and fit with people and their behaviours, rather than attempting to bend people to fit into rigid processes.

A great example of understanding the human element of processes was the time I was called in my capacity as an on-call duty manager in the early hours of one morning. The report given to me was that millions of customers were affected by the 'diggy' product being down. I had no reference to this product anywhere in my documentation, and I struggled to even know who to connect with to find out more as the reference was so obscure. It eventually transpired that it was a client in China who used an API for one of our services and that the API connection was not responding. Having clear, comprehensive terms documented is the difference between effective, rapid support, and delayed ineffective support, especially during a major incident."

From a Service Management Practitioner's Perspective

Lucy Grimwade (she/her)
Enterprise Service Management Consultant

"The reputation of a good service management professional is often deemed as a tough one to define. With the ask of a person to be unrealistically a 'jack or jill of all, and master of all', which includes, but is not limited to, technical background, being cool under pressure and juggling multiple things at once. All, of course, are good qualities to have. However, I would like to challenge those 'familiar' asks and some of the misconceptions about the profession.

When I think of what makes a good service management professional – I immediately think of three power skills:

1. ***Understanding the voice of the customer***

9: What makes a great service management professional?

Understanding what your customer (whether internal or external) experience, including their needs, wants, expectations and preferences can ultimately define the success of a service that is provided.

2. ***Being curious while co-creating relationships***
   Curiosity stops you from jumping to conclusions. It also enables collaboration and stronger root-cause analysis and sustainability when implementing new or improved change.
3. ***Leading with an entrepreneurial mindset***
   When leading with an entrepreneurial mindset, you are enabling yourself to discover and uncover opportunities, develop resilience and define success that is relevant to you and the business.

To summarise, while having enough technical knowledge can be seen as a benefit, the profession requires more of a holistic approach that is beyond process. A good service management professional utilises their power skills, which tend to be more people- and customer-centric."

From a Service Management Practitioner's Perspective

Matt Beran
Host of Ticket Volume Podcast, InvGate Product Specialist, IT Fan

"Given my previous claims that all businesses are doing service management, a professional studies the way that successful businesses improve services. Therefore, a great professional is able to connect the study of service management into practical methods of applying it to their own teams and situations.

What's so interesting to me is that these descriptions quickly highlight the importance of what many frameworks call continual service improvement (CSI). Experienced service management professionals understand and apply CSI to everything. They see teams toiling to achieve their goals and then work with those teams to imagine and design new ways of accomplishing those same achievements. Measurement and feedback are incorporated and reviewed and ultimately, the services improve.

When services improve, experiences, products and revenue often follow suit."

From a Service Management Expert's Perspective

Claire Agutter
Director at Scopism, Service Management Author and Host of The ITSM Crowd

"One of the things I notice when I talk to service management professionals is how few of them made a conscious decision to pursue a career in ITSM. I'm a typical example – I went from shopfloor retail to answering queries via a website and then to an IT helpdesk, which is where my career started. When people do find their way into ITSM, they find that it can be a rewarding, frustrating and fantastic place to be – giving rise to one of the most passionate and supportive professional communities that I know. So, who are these ITSMers? What traits do they share? Are they born, or are they made?

I would say the number one characteristic necessary for a service management professional is to care deeply about whoever is on the receiving end of your service. Whether you're making sure support calls are answered on time or developing applications that thousands of people will use, that focus on the consumer is the foundation. Building on that foundation, traits like curiosity, problem-solving, experimentation and a willingness to challenge the status quo are all typical of the people I've met and worked with. There are techniques that professionals can learn to help them along the way, but ultimately anyone who doesn't care about their consumers will not be effective in service management."

From a Service Management 'Newbie's' Perspective
Gareth Jones

Project Manager with a Background in Business Analysis

"In terms of building a career, service management contains a diverse list of roles and responsibilities that fit different skill sets. If it appeals to you, it's possible to move around different stages of the service lifecycle with clear lines of progression or diversification throughout – or you could focus your efforts in one area to specialise. But the really useful bit is to be able to move to just about any industry you want, as the basic principles of everything you have put into practice will remain the same."

From a C-level Perspective

Daniel Breston
Retired CIO, now a Public Speaker and Board Member at the itSMF UK

Daniel writes from the perspective of a CIO or principle consultant for a large firm.

"Wow! What a loaded question! If I knew that I would be the world's best and most sought-after CIO or CHRO. Let's look at this using my favourite metric system of Good, Bad, and

Great, aka GBG. It is more difficult that the table could be drawn in many ways based on their seniority or role. So, let's do the basic individual."

Table 5: Daniel Breston (CIO) – The GB&G of a Service Management Professional

	Good	**Bad**	**Great**
"Skills	*They know what service management means and can apply it to our business.* *They know our tools.* *They understand metrics and can follow the guard rails DevOps, lean, ITSM, Agile (don't care really but they need a foundation view).* *High-level Cloud, cyber security, Office, virtual comms.*	*They knew ITSM but now just follow instructions.* *No regard to business (staff, team or customers).* *They treat metrics as bonus goals.* *They care less than I do and do not keep current with latest thinking.* *Not part of their job so they don't apply other practices to their role.*	*They challenge our use of ITSM in regard to impact (outcomes) to business (staff, customers, risk).* *They have no fear of suggesting other tools.* *They keep up with latest thinking on frameworks.* *They can create a daily metric to act as a guide for them doing 'GBG' in regard to agreed team/corporate goals.* *They test business continuity as part of every sprint or change, either actually or on paper to ensure we aren't creating a disaster.*

	Good	Bad	Great
ABC (Attitude + Behaviour = Culture)	*They care about their team.* *They want to learn.* *They suggest improvements.* *They appreciate that trying and not succeeding is not failure but the outcome of an experiment.* *They participate in 360° reviews on a weekly basis.* *They challenge respectfully.*	*They are in it for the job.* *Their view is that the manager says, and they do.* *They do not suggest improvements.* *They work best in a non-servant-leadership organisation.*	*They strive to improve everyday by asking if what they did will help the team, staff or a customer.* *They raise their hands if they feel that something is not right.* *They want to experiment and try.* *They participate in 360° reviews.* *Their goal is to reflect often (no less than every sprint) on how what they did contributed to the business.*
Ad hoc	*They want to obtain buy-in before they agree to be empowered.*	*They need help them to get a role someplace else.*	*They need encouragement to speak to the organisation as often as possible".*

From a C-level Perspective

Suraj Bithal
C-level Executive

"As a C-suite executive, there are key traits that I look for in my service management function and personnel. In today's world of agility, iterative development and consumer value, it is vital that service management's ability to work vertically and horizontally across the business is enabled in the company's operating framework.

The ability to relate to each layer of the business hierarchy opens the commonly siloed approach that exists within many companies' operating models.

To get the company to embrace a service culture, it is key that service management personnel recognise that traits such as empathy, vision and strategy, business appreciation and people skills, among many others, are critical to any successful service management department.

***Empathy** must not be underestimated, given that 80% of a service management professional's role deals with risk, incidents, service failures and under-pressure leadership. The ability to relate to the customer is centric on resolving and appeasing common tensions, especially in high-pressured environments.*

***Vision and strategy** are areas that not many hiring managers would deem to be critical to a service management function. Still, they play a key part in decision-making, metric analysis and business relationship management. Not being in sync with the team, department or leadership's aspirations could lead to conflict when applying basic service frameworks. This is where the ability to embed best practice into a company's culture or ways of working is key to success*

***Business appreciation** is necessary in any service area, whether you work in change, incident or any ITIL value-add processes. A thorough understanding of business operations, customer expectations and potential downstream/upstream impacts is a huge plus to any executive who empowers their service management leadership to drive performance and reputation.*

*Lastly, and by no means the least important (actually, one of the most important) is **people skills**. The soft skills that empower those teams around service to communicate, collaborate and feel the true value of what they are delivering. The ability to manipulate any situation and drive the agenda towards a common business goal while dealing with a multitude of different personalities is an art on its own. The presence of a multi-skilled 'enabler' of personas is of huge value to any leadership team."*

The author's perspective

I've worked in IT for this long due to a genuine desire to innovate as a technologist, and I work in 'service' due to a passion for co-creating value, which has driven me from my days as a service desk analyst to the present day as an enterprise service management consultant, speaker and author. I believe this combination of being a technologist with a willingness to act with curiosity and communicate has been pivotal to my 'success' in the role.

Service management professionals need to display a passion for technology. That passion is essential and should be aligned with a level of curiosity that provides you with the natural communicative tools required to develop relationships with your colleagues and customers, which, when well used, will give you an insight into how the technology can enable your customers.

We work in a technical space that is constantly evolving, as are ways of working and engagement; therefore, being able to keep up to date with events and share them with your audience is pivotal to your success.

How you share and how you implement are critical success factors. If I can offer one piece of advice, it's that you should work with people to develop and deploy technology solutions, and you should not do what I did in the past and over-govern those services as you will end up 'doing to' as opposed to 'working with'.

Be curious, be communicative, embrace technology as an enabler and consciously 'learn, unlearn and relearn', and you'll make a great career out of service management.

Summary

I am so privileged and thankful to have received the contributions included in this chapter and the book as a whole; I wanted to provide you with a rounded view of what makes a good service management professional, as opposed to just my opinion.

Hopefully, the content of this chapter resonates with you, either as someone making a career in service management or as a leader seeking to empower and enable your teams.

Those who have contributed did so autonomously with no intervention from me. This is critical to illustrate our common points and demonstrate how we can help one another in all circumstances as a service management community.

I wanted to summarise this chapter with another infographic as I'm a big fan of a picture; in this case, a picture is worth a thousand words. Or at least one hundred.

Figure 13 is a word cloud that attempts to sum up the contributions towards this chapter. I love how it reflects key themes that continually come up when discussing our role:

- Acting professionally.
- Being focused on people as well as technology.
- Thinking about customers and value.
- Having a curiosity and passion for our work.
- Understanding that we are delivering customer services.
- Being empathetic.

Figure 13: Service Management Professional Word Cloud

These themes are recurring because they are true. Another element that crops up is how those of us working in the industry do not always plan to arrive at these roles.

Claire Agutter discusses this topic in her submission, and that's what I'd like to lead into next – service management careers.

CHAPTER 10: SERVICE MANAGEMENT CAREERS

Elements of this book discuss how ITSM enables organisations and how ITSM is a great thing to do for your enterprise, your colleagues, customers, consumers and partners.

The role of a service management professional is essential to any business that relies on digital services or serves digital customers and consumers – which is pretty much any organisation on the planet today.

Far too many of us arrive into the role of ITSM professional without a clear path; I'd like to use this chapter to discuss the 'type' of person who can make a success of service management as a career as well as discussing how leaders can best develop and empower these people as individuals and as teams.

Anyone choosing to take up a career in ITSM will have a diverse range of options and industries to choose from. ITSM requires several skills and experiences as careers in this sector are challenging with a multitude of responsibilities and functions. For instance, if you are hired for the position of a service level manager, you will have accountability for all aspects of the company's digital services including the delivery of IT services as per business requirements, while also having scope that spans the organisational partners, customers and consumers, not to mention your colleagues within the organisation.

This chapter aims to demystify what sort of people can take on a service management career and enable any organisation to achieve its strategic intent.

T-shaped service management

As we've seen, ITSM, its career path, trajectory and skills enable organisations across the corporate hierarchy from the top down, bottom up and across. ITSM professionals are often great 'service' people, and while this is an enormous asset, they should also have or seek to have skills or at least a passion for technology and innovation.

True digital and enterprise-focused ITSM is about being passionate about sharing the knowledge developed through the lessons you've learned, successes and experiences across the organisation as a whole (the top of the T), all while also sharing these attributes from top to bottom and bottom up throughout the IT business unit (the vertical part of the T).

In this chapter, we'll discuss what's known as a 'T-shaped professional' and how this relates to service management professionals and their enablement of whole enterprises.

What is a T-shaped professional?

Over the last decades, employees have become more accustomed to breaking out of their lanes. Some may call this a side hustle; it's a way for us to explore our interests and desires and increase our skills by trying something different while committing to our core roles.

In turn, those professionals hiring and identifying talent have more widely accepted that more than one skill set makes for a desirable employee.

Job descriptions are often littered with words such as 'expertise, experience, demonstratable' or that classic of '15 years' experience in' when hiring for junior to mid-level roles. As a hiring manager myself, I recognise the 'need' for these words, but when I see a CV, I'm looking to understand how someone has applied their skills, the industries and scenarios in which they've done so, and where.

I'm looking for that T-shaped professional.

As discussed earlier in the book, IT has weaved its way into everyday life; added to this, the delivery of Information Technology services relies on the 'service' being delivered in line with the desired value-focused outcomes of those receiving the service.

Within this chapter are some key elements, namely an understanding of IT and the ability to turn it into and run it as a service. Due to the advent of IT in the workplace and beyond, many factors and valuable skills can be transferred from one role to another across different sectors – making those who hold such skills invaluable and the demand for such a trait far more sought after.

T-shaped professionals are valuable members to have on your team, and as a leader, you should be looking out for these qualities. I aim to briefly explain what a T-shaped professional is, what are considered T-shaped skills, and how to create T-shaped teams.

Broadly speaking, a T-shaped professional has specialised knowledge and skills in a particular area and the desire and ability to make connections across different disciplines. These ways of working are often critical to adapting yourself when working with clients. They don't usually care to know how you deliver excellent IT services; they want to benefit from them. Recruiting for these transferable skills makes such roles invaluable to companies, and those professionals with a combination of expertise and broad ability to learn and develop are at an advantage. As are those organisations that employ such professionals.

Luckily for us, with the proper support and guidance, each of us has the potential to grow and become more T-shaped. You, your manager, colleagues, and your customers can educate individuals on the benefits, both personal and professional, of T-shaped characteristics.

In addition to technical skills – for example, ITSM and design expertise – T-shaped people possess cognitive skills like emotional intelligence and creativity. This makes them high performers who can boost your organisation's overall productivity. Those with T-shaped characteristics can form lasting relationships and connections, contribute, and problem-solve.

With the right resources and attitude, anyone can become a T-shaped individual. If you can see that an employee already has an area of expert skill alone, you may consider helping them broaden their knowledge across other avenues. If they have a wider breadth of knowledge in several skills, you could work with them to choose one and commit to making it an area they excel in.

No matter the stage in your career or your position within an organisation, there is always an opportunity to develop yourself and those around you.

What are T-shaped skills?

Each of us naturally has different skills and abilities. Some of us may be considered a one-trick pony, contributing our expertise alone, while others seem to take to a hoard of skills – the 'jack of all trades'. A T-shaped employee falls neatly in the middle of these two opposites.

Landing on either side of the spectrum is OK; you can develop yourself with support or provide your employees with the support and resources to become more T-shaped.

As discussed, T-shaped employees are precious to any organisation.

Examples of skills evident in many T-shaped people include:

- Broad knowledge about a particular topic;
- Passion and understanding of a set of topics;
- Broader context for their specialised skill set;
- Keen interest in how humans and society work;
- Understanding of the industry they work in and the ability to discuss this; and
- Basic knowledge of how the business world works.

Soft skills – sometimes called 'interpersonal' or 'people' skills – are subjective and harder to measure – for example:

- Teamwork.
- Communication.
- Time management.
- Respect and appreciation for diversity and inclusivity.
- Tolerance and open-mindedness.

Benefits of hiring T-shaped individuals

Hiring T-shaped individuals can be very beneficial both on an individual level – perhaps as a manager – and enterprise-wide.

Core skills and the ability to learn quickly through ALOE (asking, listening, observing and empathising) are just a few reasons why T-shaped employees excel in their main responsibilities. They also perform other tasks throughout the business effectively.

Thus, they contribute to the growth of the business.

Specifically, they offer these advantages:

- **Core skills:** T-shaped employees excel in their primary responsibilities within their job roles. The deep expertise that a T-shaped employee will display to push conversations forward and encourage innovation and continual improvement is a huge benefit to the organisation.
- **Communication skills:** Due to their interpersonal skills, they can employ ALOE effectively with people, whole teams and consumers, and understand their needs – across the enterprise, its partners, customers and consumers.
- **Collaboration skills:** They can discuss matters and work well over the entire organisation using collaborative techniques that bring people together outside stressful situations. This goes hand in hand with the communicating skills above.
- **A flexible approach:** T-shaped employees are flexible enough to take on new tasks and even suggest new ways of working alongside their workload without compromising the quality of work. They can achieve their immediate goals while implementing these and any new plans as part of continual-improvement activities.
- **Holistic thinking:** Those with a specific skill set (I-shaped employees) are of great value. However, they

can often fall into optimising only their piece of the puzzle – concentrating solely on their business unit or organisational area and neglecting other areas of importance. On the other hand, T-shaped employees can apply their specialised knowledge and desire to learn across the enterprise, its partners, customers and consumers.

Developing T-shaped teams

Despite their value, T-shaped teams can be difficult to blend and create. Often, especially in IT, organisations are built from a foundation of specialist individuals and skills. This no longer needs to be the case, especially as it becomes more widely accepted that transferable people and skills are key contributors to success.

Research suggests that the average UK worker will change employer every five years. In IT, I suggest this looks more like 18–24 months.[11]

T-shaped teams add value to the wider organisation, enabling the organisation to do the following:

- Provide agile ways of working that blend techniques with a focus on value.
- Enable staff to work cross-functionally with a balanced approach to their formation and growth.

---

[11] *https://www.bbc.co.uk/news/business-38828581*.

- Promote diversity and inclusion. This benefit can be realised by combining skills and expertise from different people from different walks of life.
- Give employees the ability to rotate their projects and develop their own workstreams that add value, thus reducing the likelihood of them becoming bored in just one rigid day-to-day role.
- Improve stability and security as T-shaped teams work with one another to motivate and innovate.
- Provide greater collaboration across the enterprise, its partners, customers and consumers.
- Breed innovation and enable the organisation to pivot when demands are placed upon it in VUCA (volatile, uncertain, complex or ambiguous) scenarios. As most recently seen during the COVID-19 pandemic.

As with everything in this book, this is not an exhaustive set of bullets and is open to interpretation. Each of these points and more can help your team and the wider enterprise to become more collaborative and productive, which will benefit everyone.

Talking or writing about T-shaped teams is a lot easier than building one – but nothing good is ever easy. You may get lucky and end up with a team of flawless 'T-like' individuals, but in the real world, I'd lay a bet that this will take some time and effort, but I'd also bet that it will be worth it.

Much of my experience and the experience of the organisations I've worked in and with would recommend that you begin by 'starting where you are'; you should try to understand what employee types you have already and their given skills.

Once you understand this, you can begin to focus on those positives that you currently have within your team and build on the areas that require development. You should do this with an end goal in mind, as developing a team relies on having an aim that everyone understands and wants to achieve.

A key element of starting where you are is to work out a way that works for you and your team to conduct self-assessments. You could ask your team to rate their confidence in certain topics. After this, you must then determine:

- Where you want staff to improve their knowledge and ability;
- How this would look for their career paths;
- What level of skill should be maintained, and how you can empower them to use it;
- What you want to add to the team by increasing the breadth of knowledge;
- Any areas you feel would benefit from specialist expertise; and
- Consider how all of this enhances the value provided to you, your team, your organisation as a whole, its partners, customers and consumers.

Encourage and indeed empower your employees to develop a mix of both soft and hard skills; these are invaluable and allow for greater transferable talents. You should regularly measure progress and ensure regular communications via one-to-ones and larger sessions that communicate across the organisation where relevant.

Encouraging growth in breadth and depth of knowledge will be hugely beneficial for your team members on an individual level as well as for everyone else. A team that possesses a mix of skills is far more likely to be motivated and successful – lending itself to a more diverse and stable workforce. If your team holds a range of skills, your organisation will be more able to:

- Minimise silos, reducing the likelihood of teams working 'against' one another;
- Increase collaboration and results in fewer challenges with coordination and differing priorities;
- Broaden and deepen knowledge and understanding over time through collaboration;
- Reduce handoffs between knowledge silos, improving the delivery of knowledge that is more maintainable, accessible and shareable; and
- Foster ownership, innovation and the ability to pivot in a VUCA world.

Jack of all trades, master of none

Over the years, I've heard the following question about employing service management professionals:

Aren't we just getting a 'jack of all trades' and, therefore, a master none?

When this has been presented to the leaders I work with, it's been intended as a negative. *"When you hear the phrase 'jack of all trades', what judgment does your mind make?"*[12] Do you also come up with negative connotations?

Maybe you see one of those amusing contestants from the BBC's "The Apprentice" – you know the type: a bit of a *"wheeler-dealer who will sell anything to anyone."*[13] Someone who knows a little bit about everything and, in doing so, uses it to get their own way. Somebody with a complete lack of specialist skills and knowledge, who'll just get involved and give it a try.

I think it's fair to say that 'jack of all trades' has become somewhat of an insult, and it's been used so many times that way in my presence that I thought it *was* one. Only through researching this book did I discover that this was not its intended meaning.

My research suggests that *"the phrase was originally used to describe a playwright who was always hanging around the theatres."*[14] This playwright *"would help with the stage, the set and the costumes."*[15] He would also listen in to performances and remember lines, and try his hand at directing when afforded the opportunity.

And here is the funny thing – at least to the undereducated in such proverbs (i.e. me and my lack of GCSEs) – this so-

---

[12] *https://www.forbes.com/sites/jodiecook/2021/05/13/why-being-a-jack-of-all-trades-is-essential-for-success/?sh=109bb0151c45*.

[13] Ibid.

[14] Ibid.

[15] Ibid.

called 'jack of all trades' was allegedly none other than one William Shakespeare.

It turns out the full phrase was as follows:

"A jack of all trades is a master of none, but oftentimes better than a master of one."

It was, in fact a compliment.

I consider myself a jack of all trades. People often use the words 'ITIL expert' or 'ITSM expert' when they approach me, but the truth is that I just have bundles of experience, and I've made hundreds if not thousands of mistakes, that I've learned from. I wouldn't call myself an 'author', but this will be my second book. My theory is that being a jack of all trades (relevant to enterprise service management) has brought me down this path.

The vast majority of my roles for the first half of my career lacked any real planning. In my careers podcast "ITs all about Choices", my guests have pretty much all said the same – and these are some successful people.

It's not that I'm saying picking an area and learning it inside-out is the wrong way to begin a specialist career; I'm saying that through trying many things and stepping out of your comfort zone, you can lead yourself on a voyage of self-discovery. Through doing this, you can gain a better understanding of your strengths and weaknesses very quickly. There is nothing wrong in discovering a weakness; if or when you do, you can set yourself on a path to improve in this area or at least learn to avoid doing it in the future.

In my case, while working at IBM, I found that exploring and experiencing different paths in such a large organisation gave me the confidence to leave home and move to London to take up a different role. Had I not done this, I would have gone on a holiday to Greece with my friends at this time. I'd have had a great time, but the reality is that I'd have returned home a week later, and nothing would have changed.

Challenging myself and taking on something new led me to discover a world of opportunity and to meet my now wife of 20 years. This was not a choice per se; it was due to my thinking, "I'll give it a go."

Since then, I have kept my eyes and ears open to opportunities, coupled with an appetite to learn. If you are working in service management, I advise you to do the same, as it enables you to grow in so many areas, builds self-awareness and confidence, and develops your brand outwardly to your network. Networking and the ability to communicate are key skills for any service management professional in today's world.

As is having a grasp of as many concepts as you can find. This enables you to deliver blended approaches or 'right practice', and a decent proficiency in multiple skills can allow for flexibility in your life and career.

I now work as an enterprise service management consultant, and I've learned that I get bored easily; my own barometer is approximately 12 months. It's only through working in and around multiple organisations that I can pivot my way from designing a process to delivering a strategy or building a careers framework – or writing a book.

I enjoy being able to operate between different functions, and the most successful service management professionals I've seen across the last 30 years seem to share the same enjoyment. They don't just operate in IT; they work across departments and even organisational ecosystems adapting and dovetailing between them.

The natural curiosity of a service manager professional enables you to find out how other departments function, how you could help each other. It also enables you to adapt your approach to all sorts of needs and pivot as necessary. Bringing that curiosity to work makes you better at doing it and adds variety. In my case, this means that I'm rarely, if ever, bored.

From a career perspective, I'd suggest that companies want to hire useful people who can adapt to situations and deliver great outcomes. This skill set should most probably be in every service management professional job description.

Another area where service management is misunderstood is within the start-up sector. An ability to work across organisational functions, deal with partners, communicate and scale service management practices are skills that can stimulate growth. Sadly, most start-ups see service management as just governance and control, and we need to change that view to be one of organisational innovation and enablement.

Put simply; broader knowledge leads to greater understanding and better advising of clients and employers across multiple areas. It's not adequate to specialise and turn a blind eye to other influences; this approach can deliver great blended approaches.

Being a 'jack of all trades' also leads you on a path to challenging yourself and others with constant professional development, which is so incredibly important in this ever-changing world.

You also get to meet people who know more than you and take on their knowledge. From here, you can use your service management skills to categorise this knowledge and, where relevant, share it and make it appropriately accessible and sustainable for others to learn from.

Being a master of every service management practice is obviously your goal as a service management professional. What good is this if you are closed off to other approaches, methods or ways of working, or to challenging yourself to try new things?

It's these skills that mean your work has a chance to reach across organisations and improve people's lives, not just your own! To close, I'd hope we've switched the T-Shape professional from being a negatively viewed Jack of all Trades to someone with a great and ever-improving working knowledge of many areas. This makes you a skilled service management professional and one who makes your hiring manager or customer feel like they've done the most incredible thing by securing your services.

Service management career paths

What is a service management career path? I'm still not sure, and I've been working in IT 'service'-related roles for 30 years and in 'core' service management roles for 23 years.

Does that mean there isn't a path? I'm not sure it does, but I think it requires development and a little more formalisation. Here is my career thus far:

My roles have included the following:

- Service desk analyst.
- Service desk leader.
- Problem manager.
- Customer satisfaction and continual improvement leader.
- Major incident manager.
- Service management process writer.
- Change manager.
- Knowledge manager.
- Problem, incident, major incident and change leader.
- Service transition leader.
- Service designer.
- Head of service management.
- Service management consultant.
- Independent service management consultant.
- Enterprise service management consultant.

In my opinion, having gone through all of these roles, it's difficult to see a path, and that's coming from me, the person that trod this path.

Have I mastered service management's equivalent of a 'jack of all trades'? I think this book proves that I'm no William Shakespeare, but maybe I have touched on the full quotation: *"A jack of all trades is a master of none, but oftentimes better than a master of one."*

I think that's a good definition of a well-rounded service management professional.

In Figure 14, I've chosen to articulate my path using an infographic.

For this purpose, I leant upon a digital service lifecycle to (I hope) demonstrate the breadth of my accountability in that role at that time. I've left out my earliest roles as these were roles I fell into predominantly. They may have been a pathway to the year 2000, but they were a series of stumbles instead of steps.

To begin my career journey, head to 'Start here:' at the bottom right of the infographic.

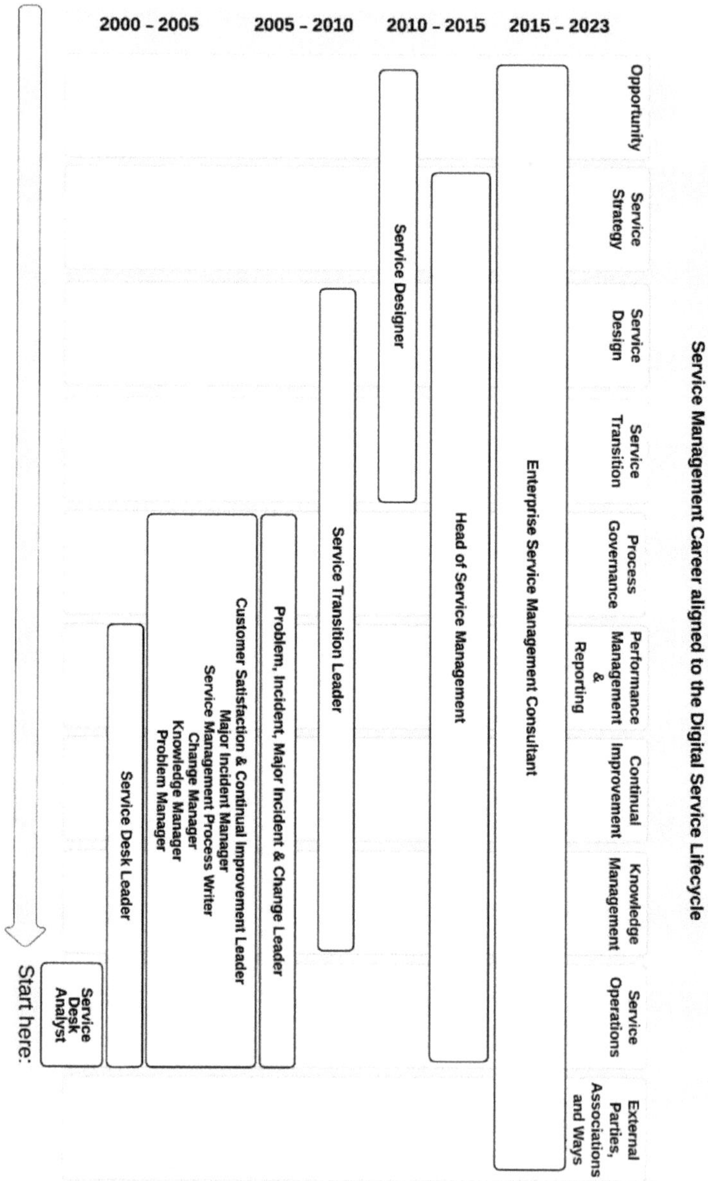

Figure 14: The Author's Career Path

Representing a career path spanning 23 years felt like quite the challenge when I began designing the infographic; I hope what we have here is easy to read and digest and less challenging than designing it in the first place.

Below are some points that I think are worth making.

- My first role as a service desk analyst remains my favourite due to its focus on day-to-day service operations.
- Trying out various service management roles helped me discover what I wanted to do and gave me T-shaped skills.
- IBM offered me many opportunities. It definitely helped me on my career path.
- The choices you make are not irreversible. You can go back, pivot or simply admit it's the right role at the wrong time (as with my role as service desk leader).
- Working in service operations was great preparation for being as a service transition leader.
- Being a service designer taught me how to give the marketing and sales teams the knowledge they needed to sell products and services more appropriately, and how to treat suppliers as partners.
- As head of service management, I was too preoccupied with my services to offer the best advice and action.
- As a consultant, I can apply what I've learned across the whole digital service lifecycle by shifting value left into the strategic and opportunity phases.

- As a consultant, I am able to study, write and join industry organisations, and become a mentor. I also get to work with my first love – the service desk.

When embracing something new, it doesn't need to be a new role or job; it could be a new way of working, a new tool, or a new location to work from (with your current employer or a new one).

You also need an employer to provide these opportunities – but they will not do so if you don't show an appetite. Sadly, we rarely get handed what we want on a plate; we need to work for it and work smart. Working smart in my book (this one) means positioning yourself around opportunities and maximising your chances of realising them.

Leaders and employers – empower your people. If they get a service management certification, empower them to deliver what they've learned, engage them and motivate them – work with them to co-create a path to success and encourage others to listen to them. If you don't, their service management career path will take them elsewhere, possibly to a competitor.

It is also important to recognise that different individuals can contribute different levels of expertise and build their careers appropriately.

Working with and building a team filled with individuals that possess a common broad base of skills and who also excel individually in particular speciality areas will benefit both the individuals and the organisation tremendously as it will retain their skills as part of a digital careers framework.

A digital careers strategy and framework can be used to determine the knowledge and skills that team members need to understand the role they play within the organisation (or aspire to play within the organisation), along with expected behaviours, and be used to engage them and retain their services.

Summary

My service management career has taken me across six employers, including my limited company, but this isn't even half the story. I've worked with 27 organisations (that I can recall). Each of them has contributed to my career and progression, as have the hundreds, if not thousands, of colleagues and customers I've worked with.

Some people have empowered me, many have trusted me, and the vast majority have positively influenced my career. Without this trust and encouragement, I would not have felt comfortable challenging myself – and those people to improve the digital services we deliver to global clients. It is so important to support one another and act as allies when needed.

I think I'm proof that trying new things, taking on challenges and pushing yourself along with a large dose of luck plus lessons learned is the key to a successful service management career – and I only imagine it's going to get better for those of you working in the industry today.

#itsallaboutchoices

CHAPTER 11: SERVICE MANAGEMENT CERTIFICATIONS

Compared to when I started in the industry, service management qualifications are ten to the penny today.

In the early noughties, I was led to pursue ITIL certification since it seemed like the most logical course to take. This road served me well and provided an excellent foundation; at least, that's how I felt at the time (*foundation pun intended).

Since then, through a mixture of my roles and training/certification, my knowledge of service management methodologies has increased along with my knowledge and experience in the field.

I will cover as many of those certifications as I can think of that are readily available at the time of writing, Q1 2023.

The hashtag #AlwaysLearning is used by an ex-client and a wonderful customer. I think it's a crucial skill for any professional, let alone a service management professional. I say this to avoid the idea that I am endorsing the certificates that follow in any particular order of preference. All of these are beneficial, and working with other professionals with alternative certifications is even more beneficial.

For more on that, see "Why I Loathe Service Management"!

I believe you should try and blend these qualifications wherever the opportunity allows. If you are a leader of a team, send your team out to several of these certifications, and on their return, invite them to work together on what they've learned and challenge them to implement these in your enterprise.

If you are a service management professional, do the courses you want and then learn from others. These certifications are rarely, if ever, opposed to one another – but when they are not adapted correctly, they can be implemented in opposition to one another.

What follows are those certification areas that I believe service management professionals should work with and on to increase their subject matter expertise. Note that this is just my opinion. Please do your own investigations based on this.

- **ITIL:** ITIL is the most universally known of the service management qualifications; that said, ITIL is not ITSM. ITIL is not something that can be complied with. Be forewarned that I've seen statements suggesting 'ITIL compliance' far too many times.
  ITIL4 is built on the fantastic foundations of previous versions, ITIL, ITIL v2 and ITIL v3. It was been brought up to the fourth industrial revolution in 2019 and beyond via the ITIL4 curriculum.
  ITIL4 Foundation is in practically every service management job description. If you go on this path, I recommend you go beyond Foundation and head towards the advanced perspectives of Practice Manager, Managing Professional and Strategic Leader. You can get much more information about ITIL at *https://www.axelos.com*, including information on how and why you'll need to recertify or add Continual Development Points to maintain your certification.

- **VeriSM:** This came to me in the months just before the ITIL4 release. It changed my way of thinking about service management.
  VeriSM moved me from ITSM to enterprise service management. Some amazing experts in service management put together VeriSM (like ITIL), which stands for **V**alue **D**riven, **E**volving, **R**esponsive **Service Management**. These are words organisations and board members understand.
  I once had to do a literal elevator pitch on the benefits of service management to a C-level professional. In those 30 seconds, I pointed out how service management co-creates Value, a value that Evolves and Responds to organisational needs, and a value that is so much more than just IT. He was sold, and we were able to use these principles to build a whole enterprise service management function over the next 15 months. It's a real shame VeriSM is not yet a prerequisite for all service management roles as, in my opinion, it's great and teaches you some strong business skills. You can learn more about VeriSM at: *https://verism.global/*.
- **SIAM**: SIAM stands for Service Integration and Management. It's about implementing a strategy to manage multiple suppliers, ensuring they have end-to-end commercials, principles and objectives. This leads to a single, integrated business-facing IT organisation. SIAM is powerful stuff and is a real organisational enabler.

I'd thoroughly recommend you go to *https://www.scopism.com/* to learn more or join the SIAM community via this link: *https://scopism.circle.so/home*.

- **VeriSM and SIAM:** These are closely aligned with the EXIN Digital Service Manager career path and the skills assessment platform Astride. Visit Astride at *https://www.exin.com/astride-by-exin/* and take the self-assessment. As a leader, you can ask your team to do this and identify areas of strength and potential improvement concerning digital skills. This is a free-to-use service which, when complete, will assess you against industry benchmarks and recommend training.
  As a team member, it can highlight where you can uplift your skills, and also recommends non-EXIN products. You can learn more about the EXIN career paths at: *https://www.exin.com/career-paths/*.
- **Agile ADapT**: Adapting frameworks to work together is a fine art keenly applied by my mentor Johann Botha (who has kindly provided a foreword this book). Johann has used his incredible expertise and experiences to develop the Agile ADapT framework. I've been fortunate enough to get an early view of this work and was the world's first certified Agile ADapT professional – something I'm very proud of.

  "Agile ADapT® is an easy & straight-forward digital business transformation approach that any organization can use to develop organizational

agility, innovate at scale, be more customer responsive and to maximally leverage technology.

Use a simple 9-step process to figure out what your customers want. Then see how you can create, build and offer new and exciting products and services that maximize customer value!"[16]

You can learn more here: https://agile-adapt.com/.

- **Humanising IT**: Put together by one of the ITIL4 authors and service management guru Katrina Macdermid, who brings her human-centred design philosophy to the party. Humanising IT is a fantastic educational piece that bridges the gap between technology and its application with human-centred design – putting people at the heart of technology. For me, it hits the sweet spot that we've been missing for years; often, we 'do to' customers, and this course helps us 'work with' customers to deliver great digital service experiences.
  You can learn more here: https://hitglobal.services/.

  At this point, we reach the end of those areas I am certified in, but that does not mean there is nothing else to study. From my perspective, I'd also suggest you look into the following areas:

- **ISO/IEC 20000**: ISO/IEC 20000 is an international standard to *"establish, implement, maintain and*

[16] https://agile-adapt.com/.

continually improve a service management system". It provides a 'compliance' view regarding how you have or will implement ITSM in your organisation. Although I am not qualified in ISO, I am a member of its international service management committee. ISO really is committed to delivering excellence and innovation across our industry, and I have great faith in these standards. To learn more, follow the link below or feel free to contact me on *david@solsevenstudio.com*. *https://www.iso.org/standard/70636.html*.

- **COBIT®**: COBIT is *"A framework for the governance and management of enterprise information and technology, aimed at the whole organisation".*
For more information, click:
https://www.isaca.org/resources/cobit.
- **IT4IT™**: IT4IT is a *"tool for aligning and managing a Digital Enterprise"*. It's an Open Group standard. For more information, click:
https://www.opengroup.org/it4it.

There are also other areas you may like to study to build a more rounded or T-shaped skill set; they will almost certainly make your life easier as a service management professional and provide you with a level of knowledge that enables you to empathise with colleagues and customers alike.

- **Agile**: Agile is a predominantly project management methodology focused on breaking a project up and delivering its requirements into phases or bite-sized chunks. AGILE is built around stakeholder collaboration and continual improvement. More info at: *https://www.exin.com/agile-devops-lean/exin-agile-scrum/exin-agile-scrum-foundation/*.

- **DevOps**: DevOps is focused on product and application development (every product or application being a service). Its main aims are centred around evolving and improving products at a faster pace than would usually be possible in organisations. This increase in velocity brings services to market with more speed than usual while DevOps maintains the standards required by the organisation. For more information, click: *https://www.exin.com/agile-devops-lean/exin-devops/exin-devops-foundation/*.
- **PRINCE2**: PRINCE2 is a structured project management method and practitioner certification programme. It emphasises dividing projects into manageable and controllable stages, often using what is known as a 'Waterfall' approach. For more information, click: *https://www.prince2.com/uk/what-is-prince2*.
- **Lean**: Lean IT is the application of 'Lean' principles to the IT domain. *"Lean is a way of thinking about creating needed value with fewer resources and less waste. And lean is a practice consisting of continuous experimentation to achieve perfect value with zero waste."*[17] For more information, click:

[17] *https://www.lean.org/explore-lean/what-is-lean/*.

https://www.exin.com/agile-devops-lean/exin-lean-it/exin-lean-it-foundation/.

- **Lean Six Sigma:** *"Lean Six Sigma is a project management technique that combines the waste reduction (Munda) principles of Lean and the focus on capability and reducing variation in Six Sigma. Combined, Lean Six Sigma combines problem-solving and continuous improvement to deliver even more outstanding results."*[18]

Service management professional designations

Did you know that you can get letters after your name when working in service management?

I had no idea until I'd worked in service management for approximately 20 years. I wish I'd found out earlier as I believe these would have reset my thinking and aims. Hopefully, I can shortcut this understanding for you.

To gain letters after your name, or – as they are professionally known – a 'suffix,' you can also seek to obtain an accredited status to illustrate your knowledge and professionalism from the likes of the BCS (British Computer Society).

- **BCS Professional membership (MBCS)**: If you're a skilled, ethical IT professional looking to raise your profile and career potential, I'd recommend checking out the British Computer Society (The BCS).

[18] *https://www.exin.com/agile-devops-lean/exin-lssa-lean-six-sigma/.*

You can choose to join the BCS as a Professional (MBCS) member, which enables you to display the suffix MBCS after your name. This will identify you as a professional who wants to be part of the driving force behind today's global technology industry. *https://www.bcs.org/membership-and-registrations/become-a-member/professional-membership/*

- **BSC Chartered IT Professional (CITP)**: This is the independent standard of competence and professionalism in the technology industry. The title Chartered IT Professional is aligned with the Skills Framework for the Information Age (SFIA), the UK-government-backed competency framework. It's the equivalent of a chartered accountant (as an example). It's an excellent qualification to achieve, as it's endorsed by a royal charter. *https://www.bcs.org/membership-and-registrations/get-registered/chartered-it-professional/*
- **BCS Fellowship of the BCS (FBCS):** *"BCS Fellowship is home to the most influential professionals in the digital industry. Connect with the leaders who share your passion for tech, technical expertise, business acumen, ethics and social responsibilities."* *https://www.bcs.org/membership-and-registrations/become-a-member/bcs-fellowship/*

Summary

The certifications and accreditations discussed in this section should be enough to keep you going for many years and will absolutely stretch your brainpower and your budget.

My advice is to take what interests you and keep an eye on the future, as I'd expect things will have moved on, especially if you find yourself reading this book in 2028. However, I'd expect the likes of CITP and FBCS to be just as important – if not more so in the coming years.

Added to all of this, be curious, open-minded, and committed to lifelong learning for your teams and for yourself.

One more vitally important point that every service management professional and leader should bear in mind: Please do not be tribal in your approach. Take something from each of these certifications and practices and share what you find with others; use value-focused CoPs to share and blend techniques that deliver strategic and value-led outcomes.

CHAPTER 12: APPLYING YOUR SERVICE MANAGEMENT CERTIFICATIONS

As well as avoiding being 'tribal', I would recommend not being 'a loner'. Completing a training course and achieving the certification is just the first step on the journey, not the final one.

When you return from training, everything you've learned will be fresh in your mind. When you achieve your passing mark is when you are most enthused. Take this energy and harness it to begin the next steps in improving yourself and the digital services you deliver.

I've talked about how I misapplied my learning in the past, focusing solely on governance and being risk-averse. I did this because I saw where my training and certification could help, but I did so in isolation.

When you return from training, discuss what you learned with others; if you manage a team, ask your team members to do the same. Form a community of people and discuss how you can apply the learning to known organisational challenges or how you can apply innovative tools and concepts.

If each of you has taken different certifications (something I'd recommend a leader arrange), challenge one another. Discuss how you could blend your thinking and the methods you've learned to apply them in a manner that can benefit your organisation.

Do not leave your certification on the metaphorical shelf; discuss it wherever you can and challenge it. Seek out others with the same certification and discuss how they have applied it.

You should also complete continual professional development (CPD) in relation to your certification and use this to motivate yourself to develop. There are global skills and competency frameworks, such as the SFIA (*https://sfia-online.org/en*), that you can use to benchmark yourself and your team members. Not to mention Astride from EXIN, as discussed in the previous chapter.

Once settled on your path, you can apply elements of your certifications by joining a professional body such as BCS or the itSMF UK to learn from others and express your knowledge and opinion. As a member of both, I can thoroughly recommend joining, and I'd love to see you on the BCS ITSM or ITAM committees one day.

If you join the committee and can recite this passage of the book, dinner's on me!

As well as joining these organisations, you can also use the membership and the opportunities it offers to mentor others.

You could choose to push yourself down the varying levels of membership and accreditation offered by the likes of the BCS. These often involve demonstrating your practical experiences and gaining support from your colleagues; they are a true and worthwhile demonstration of your skills and experience.

You do not need these accreditations to mentor others, but I found that having them gave me the confidence to do so. It also attracted mentees to engage me in the hope that I could help them develop into these accreditations. This is not a trust I take lightly.

Mentoring is incredibly rewarding for all parties, and it's something that I believe really lends itself to applying your certification through coaching others, discussing your and their learnings and ultimately giving something back. Mentoring is not 'easy', and it takes time, but I consider it the most rewarding aspect of my job.

You could even challenge yourself to speak or write about your learning and how you apply it. Speaking and writing about service management is difficult as you open yourself up to critique – something I've not always been comfortable with. It challenges your confidence, but also connects you to a network of great people who can give feedback and help you improve.

My imposter syndrome is a constant, and writing this book is a massive challenge, but I really hope that it will help other service management professionals. These aspects inspire me to challenge myself – and there is no doubt that it's incredibly rewarding; I would thoroughly recommend it.

Summary

'Just do it' is a slogan for a well-known sportswear brand. It fits my perspective on service management certification and the need to apply these appropriately in your organisation and across YOUR career. A career that I hope will take you across many industries facing a series of ever more complex challenges.

'Just doing it' should not mean doing something in an isolated or singular fashion. It means you should, wherever possible, blend approaches, work with people who may have opposing views, and in fact, seek them out and work together to deliver a blended approach that stimulates and innovates.

Please do not do what I did and blindly apply the certification by the book and disable yourself, your organisation, its customers, consumers and partners. You will not be thanked, and ultimately you will not thank yourself.

Commit to 'learn, unlearn and relearn' and #Alwayslearning. These are merely phrases, but it's only through continual learning that we can grow. This, combined with our communication skills, often allows us to retain relevance and be offered new and exciting opportunities.

Service management certifications teach you business skills, not just IT skills. Those accreditations are proof that you can apply these skills, so go and apply them.

Don't just apply them to ITSM. Use them to contribute towards the success of the enterprise as a whole. From there, share your learning, help others to develop and give back; your actions will deliver a greater impact if you work this way.

CHAPTER 13: WHY I LOATHE SERVICE MANAGEMENT – TALES FROM THE AUTHOR

In one word: Tribalism. In my 30 years of experience, I'm yet to go to an organisation where I don't see an element of tribalism. People tend to be in the DevOps tribe, the ITIL tribe or the Agile tribe, and that's before we find the IT, the HR tribe and the sales tribe.

Even when we create a CoP to overcome this, that itself involves a bunch of like-minded people unwittingly forming a tribe focused on value. We are doing it for the right reasons, but our tribal nature is often what limits our success.

In the business world, even when we are in the same organisation, we often find ourselves at cross-purposes with our colleagues from different departments or areas.

Sales and marketing teams want the flexibility to meet changing customer demands, while product development and technology teams need stability to drive scale and efficiency.

Departments and subsidiaries in different countries or regions want solutions specific to their unique markets. At the same time, corporate headquarters require all units to align to a single, clear strategy, and often this strategy is not communicated appropriately.

Centres of expertise are set up to create long-range, big-picture, innovative strategies to help client-facing employees who typically want immediate fixes for customer pain points as they often feel the 'pain' of a negative customer experience first.

And among all of this, we have the suppliers or partners who are working towards their own organisational goals while attempting to fit in with yours.

Even if everyone is on the same side, our daily goals and needs are different. As a result, you find mindsets that reflect more an 'us versus them' rather than 'us versus our competitors' attitude.

As a result, communication loses its effectiveness, and the teams begin to drift from one another. This is when things start to go tribal.

Even though this is not a service management issue per se, it is an issue that can impact the effectiveness of service management and other enterprise functions across the organisation.

Typical symptoms that are seen in this scenario are:

Lobbing stuff over the fence: I'm hoping that the term 'lobbing' translates easily. It means throwing something and not caring if anyone is there to catch it. Usually, this behaviour results in teams blaming one another, criticising the others' work, or continually throwing work over the fence from design into operation with huge gaps that impact the consumers.

I've seen this get so bad that a team was been placed on a watchlist and ordered to undertake a digital-change embargo. This effectively meant that they could not maintain or change a digital service in line with customer requirements. Unfortunately, only the customer suffers in this scenario.

What made this worse was that the team under said embargo just carried on but was ignored, but they did so in the name of delivering to their customer.

Even more frustrating was that they were doing some incredible work, but nobody engaged with them to find out more and ask 'why'. This was a double-edged sword; they were perceived to be 'lobbing' stuff over the fence, but tribalism caused those receiving the service to ostracise them, which only exasperated the issue

Blaming the customer: This occurs all too frequently. It's especially frustrating as it's usually a communication issue, much like the example above.

And so it was in this case. Eventually, the one common ground both teams shared was to apportion blame to the customer for not being clear in their requirements, even though these were documented and signed off.

On investigation and with a little conversation, it was deduced that over-engineered processes and governance structures caused this situation. None of this was helped by a lack of inter-team communication and misaligned objectives that came from poorly thought-out leadership.

In this scenario, a one-hour meeting pretty much resolved an issue that had been impacting customers for almost a year.

We don't work that way: This is perhaps the most severe case of tribalism, especially in ITSM. It's when whole departments or organisations refuse to cooperate with one another based on their methodology or practice, claiming 'We are DevOps', 'We are ITIL', or 'We are Agile'.

'We' often seem to miss that you can blend methodologies, and ultimately, we should work together and use the 'right practice' for our organisation and not blindly follow one way of working like some sort of faith.

Working this way can go as far as developing a culture of mistrust. You can find your organisation rewarding this lack of cooperation between hundreds of people in the same company as objectives are completely misaligned with one another and the organisational strategy.

Even more amusing or toe-curling is when working together across departments to find a joint solution is seen to be collaborating with the enemy!

I've honestly seen this, where different departments have long, animated and frightfully non-conclusive discussions around who 'owns' the customer and when. These kinds of conversations led to nobody 'owning' the customer, and as a result, the customer was left out of the loop entirely. We end up with a digital service that fails to hit the customer's value-based outcomes.

Summary

Nobody and nothing is perfect, least of all IT or enterprise service management. But if it was perfect, we'd be out of work and bored. Embrace the challenge and turn loathing into love.

Having seen these past misbehaviours and cases of tribalism enables me to say that I think things are beginning to change, which allows me to start to discuss and go into what I love about service management as an organisational enabler.

CHAPTER 14: WHY I LOVE SERVICE MANAGEMENT

I believe that tribalism can be attributed to poor leadership and a poorly communicated or thought-out strategy. Too often, strategic objectives are like unicorns – awesome, but they don't exist. So, I've laid the blame at the leaders' doors…or have I?

In truth, we all have a responsibility to act professionally. This means getting to grips with the organisational strategy, feeding back to leadership if you are unclear on the strategy, and managing up, across and down the organisation.

As service management professionals, we are at the cross-section of organisations where we dovetail between technology, product development, marketing, HR, the board etc., which is why I love working in this area. I especially love it when the service management focus is encouraged at the enterprise level.

Each one of us is responsible for communicating appropriately; we should be human-centric in our behaviour and respect our colleagues, customers, consumers and partners.

Enterprise-focused service management is not just an operating function. Although we are not 'the organisation', we represent so many aspects of an organisation that we can be incredibly influential in stepping towards solving organisational issues that manifest themselves in poorly delivered and supported digital services.

When these issues occur, whole organisations suffer financial and reputational loss; the following are reasons I love Service Management framed through the solutions it can offer to the elements I loathe.

Goals and objectives: I cannot stress the importance of this area. SLAs should not be 'watermelon' in their design and delivery, and they should not lead teams down conflicting paths that result in unhappy customers and consumers. Goals and objectives should be aligned, and wherever possible, they should focus on value to the organisational strategy, its employees, customers, consumers and even its partners.

Wherever possible, use enterprise service management principles to link goals, objectives and service levels to the holistic vision and always retain an awareness of the organisational-level goals. If teams oppose one another, reset this by re-emphasising those organisational goals and their alignment with service levels.

Communicate, recommunicate: This is the leader's responsibility, and I'd add senior service management professionals into the mix.

Step out of these 'firefights' and seek to frame the situation for those whom you lead or who follow. Be careful with defining the mission or goal for the teams aiming to attain and achieve the goals. If collaboration or a new way of working is essential, then say so, using as many channels as possible and be incredibly consistent in what you say and when you say it. Always invite feedback on this and act upon it as openly as possible. This empathises the power of open speech, developing trust and buy-in at all levels.

Break down silos: Geographical boundaries no longer stop us from being 'together', though they do not replace being together. Use multiple methods and communication channels to bring teams together. Expertise, knowledge and skills are widely distributed across the enterprise and its geographical locations; therefore, you must use everything you have to break down information and data silos to be competitive, and innovate as appropriate about your strategic goals.

Service management can act as an enterprise function, using CoPs to bring teams together (do not form a tribe, though) to bridge gaps in knowledge, understanding, objectives and communication, and blend approaches to deliver value-driven outcomes. A CoP can take regular temperature checks, working against a charter focused on reducing silos, improving communication, and measuring success in these areas.

When I first began working as a consultant, I was offered some advice: to use my experience to spot the problem in the organisational hierarchy and then look one level above. This has served me well and placed me in some sticky situations! And it is why I began this chapter by blaming and then admonishing blame from organisational leaders.

Time management: Schedule some time to speak with senior leaders if you can. If they are not available to do so – that's a worry. Suppose senior leaders don't respond to invites with a clear agenda and proposed outcomes. In that case, this has a habit of becoming an organisational symptom, impacting communication as others follow their lead and fail to respond to reasonable and clearly articulated meeting requests.

All of this increases Silos, reduces knowledge sharing and wastes time. If you can meet with senior leaders, ask them a couple of questions:

- What are the organisation's strategic goals for the next year? (This helps you understand their view on the strategy and its goals and lets you know if these are shared with other leaders.)
- What does 'value' mean to you? (This helps you understand their drivers and if these are shared with other leaders.)

From here, discuss the messages they send around value, strategic intent, objectives, collaboration and cooperation. Are these sensible? Are they getting to the correct audiences and with the desired frequency from all involved? Is everyone on the same page? It won't happen at lower levels if your senior leadership isn't displaying joined-up behaviour or sending the needed communication. Service management can help by taking on these communications, building value into digital services and ensuring they are designed with strategic goals in mind. Service management should do this as well as managing digital service operations, measurement, commercial agreements, etc., as service management should look after services end-to-end.

Using service management skills and professionalism to manage the human dynamics actively will help your organisation reap the benefits of having different speciality areas in your company while at the same time mitigating the downsides of tribalism.

I find that where I really 'love' service management is its ability to use the past to help the future. Wherever you are, in whatever organisation or department you work, I expect much of what I've discussed here to be recognisable and solvable.

Over the last eight years, I've been asked to assess organisations' service management methodologies, operations and delivery and make recommendations. Everything I've written in this chapter and this book is based on those experiences.

It's a lot to sum up, but I am often asked to do so. I enclose an infographic summarising the typical examples I've encountered and discussed in this book. This is not typical of every organisation, but elements of it are usually found during my engagements.

Figure 15: Common Service Management Recommendations

Summary

At the risk of repeating myself, I truly 'love' service management.

I love service management much the same way as my favourite football team, Liverpool FC. In service management, as in football, you cannot win every tackle, score every goal, or save every shot on goal. You certainly cannot win every match.

You go through ups and downs, elation and despair but return for more. With Liverpool, I do this because I know the vision is to win the league, the European cup, the league cup and the FA Cup. I can get behind that and the team and our manager, as I want to support this vision.

All that said, I and many others debate transfer activity, ticket costs, new kits and commercial activities because we are not always privy to the organisational strategy.

Not all organisations have an excellent scenario where they've got such clear aims and a team so visibly aiming for them, but that doesn't mean that vision and strategy should be neglected. As ITSM and especially enterprise-focused service management professionals, we can work with our leaders, our organisational colleagues, partners and customers/consumers to deliver great digital experiences that delight our consumers and fulfil our working lives.

This is the enterprise-focused service management professional equivalent of scoring the winning goals in a cup final. Ultimately, I love service management more than I loathe it.

CHAPTER 15: WHAT NEXT FOR SERVICE MANAGEMENT?

I wish I had a crystal ball, but if I did and it worked, I'd probably be looking for the lottery numbers and not thinking about the future of service management.

Alas, that is not the case.

Service management, IT, enterprises as a whole and the entire world around us are moving so fast that it's almost impossible to predict the future of service management as an industry.

Service management has taught me that we can learn much from looking backwards in preparing for our future. If there is one thing I can do, it is to use my knowledge of our evolution thus far to predict our future.

In early 2023, I was privileged to be invited by ManageEngine to discuss my three key strategic areas for service management over the next three years, as you can see in the following link:

https://www.manageengine.com/products/service-desk/itsm/service-management-strategy.html.

As per all good research papers, I was not the only one to be asked, and I, among others, discussed some exciting themes which I'll use to form this part of the book in having a stab at what the future may look like.

Some of these will be recognisable from those areas discussed earlier and those to follow.

At its core, the research agreed that service management strategies should align with the organisation and its strategic intent and needs.

Two core key areas are highlighted as common themes across the ten contributors, all built on many years of cumulative knowledge.

These areas were:

1. Addressing people-related issues and needs; and
2. Ways of working or process-related improvements.

My three strategic areas concentrated on the people side and span across processes, platforms, etc. But I begin with a more technological 'future' for service management that is very much in the present.

Service management and emerging and embedding technologies

In early 2023, we saw the relative explosion of ChatGPT as a source of information due to its ability to disseminate information speedily and seemingly pertinently when asked a question.

To me, this is just good old IT-service-management-based knowledge management. It would be remiss of me not to ask ChatGPT what it thinks the future of service management is.

It takes a more technical lead than I would have, but I think it's interesting. Everything that follows in italics was sourced from ChatGPT at: *https://chat.openai.com/chat*.

I asked it three questions.

Question one:

What is enterprise service management?

Answer: *"Enterprise Service Management (ESM) is a Service Management approach that focuses on delivering high-quality and cost-effective services to meet the needs of an organisation. It involves the use of technology, processes, and people to manage and improve the delivery of services across the Enterprise.*

ESM covers a wide range of services, including IT services, HR services, facilities management, and customer service. The goal of ESM is to provide consistent and efficient service delivery, improve service quality, and reduce costs.

ESM often uses Service Management tools and technologies such as ServiceNow, BMC Remedy, and CA Service Management to automate and streamline service delivery processes. It also relies on Service Level Agreements (SLAs) and other performance metrics to measure and improve service quality."

Question two:

Tell me about artificial intelligence in enterprise service management

Answer: *"Artificial Intelligence (AI) has been increasingly adopted in Enterprise Service Management (ESM) to automate and optimise various Service Management processes. AI-powered solutions can improve the efficiency, accuracy, and speed of tasks such as incident resolution, problem diagnosis, and service request fulfilment.*

Some applications of AI in ESM include:

1. *Chatbots and virtual assistants: AI-powered chatbots and virtual assistants can provide quick and efficient customer support, reducing the workload on human service desk agents.*
2. *Predictive analytics: AI can analyse large amounts of data to identify patterns and predict future service incidents and problems. This enables organisations to proactively address potential issues before they become problems.*
3. *Machine learning: Machine learning algorithms can be used to automate routine Service Management tasks and improve decision-making processes.*
4. *Natural language processing (NLP): NLP enables AI-powered solutions to understand and interpret human language, improving communication between service desk agents and customers.*

The integration of AI into ESM has the potential to significantly improve service quality and reduce costs. However, it is important to consider the ethical and security implications of AI in ESM and ensure that AI-powered solutions are implemented and used responsibly."

Question three:

What is the future of enterprise service management?

Answer: *"The future of Enterprise Service Management (ESM) is likely to be shaped by several emerging trends and technologies, including:*

1. *Artificial Intelligence (AI) and Machine Learning (ML): AI and ML are expected to play a significant role in the*

future of ESM, automating routine tasks and enabling service organisations to respond more quickly and effectively to customer needs.

2. *Cloud computing: The adoption of cloud computing is likely to continue to increase, enabling organisations to access ESM solutions on a pay-per-use basis and scale up or down as needed.*
3. *Internet of Things (IoT): The growth of IoT devices is expected to generate large amounts of data that can be analysed and used to improve service delivery.*
4. *Remote and hybrid work: The trend towards remote and hybrid work will likely continue, leading to increased demand for cloud-based ESM solutions that can be accessed from anywhere.*
5. *The customer experience (CX): The focus on customer experience is expected to increase, driving organisations to invest in ESM solutions that provide personalised and proactive service.*

These trends and technologies will likely drive significant changes in the ESM landscape in the coming years, leading to more efficient and effective service delivery and improved customer satisfaction."

I carried out this experiment to demonstrate how a fundamental enterprise service management principle of knowledge management has always been in play since we started typing into search engines. Our yellow pages in the 1980s and 1990s were a form of knowledge management.

In this case, all that has changed is that knowledge is more accessible and easily digestible. It now also has context as it trawls through the Internet, conducting, collating and sharing knowledge faster than a human ever could. This remains the future of service management as much as its present, as we must continually improve it to ensure it remains relevant.

In conclusion, while ChatGPT and other AI language models are changing the landscape, they are not designed to replace human context and intelligence. Instead, they are meant to be powerful tools that support and enhance our work, helping us to produce high-quality information faster and more efficiently.

Thanks, ChatGPT.

Education in service management

For this to work at an organisational level, education and examining bodies and professional bodies must work together to ensure that ITSM is accessible from an educational standpoint and usable from an enterprise perspective.

In an ideal world, we can then better demonstrate the benefits of ITSM to senior business leaders such that they can strategise the development of enterprise-focused service management. (Plus, I'd love to see a higher entry point to ITIL for C-level people).

We also need to get service management into the curriculum at high schools, colleges and universities. We are a young industry but also an old one that lacks inclusivity and diversity. I believe this is due to a lack of knowledge around service management careers being offered to young people and those studying subjects such as computer science.

Service management is a great career offering the ability to work across industries at all levels. It also offers obvious benefits such as hybrid working and well above average salaries and benefits. We need to make young people are aware of this so they can consider it as a potential career path.

Furthermore, we need an entry point for senior executives to get to know service management and the benefit it and its people offer their organisations. This book hopes to fulfil some of that, but we need a joined-up industry-wide approach to this predicament and to do this over the next three years.

Value co-creation and enterprise-focused service management

For ITSM to evolve, we must work on strategies that remove the purely 'I' element and focus on the 'service' element.

Everything we do in the digital world relates to service. Following VeriSM's lead and de-coupling ITSM from IT, 'IT' SM is an organisational enabler and must work as such. We also need to shift the focus from watermelon SLAs to the 'experience' focus of experience level agreements (XLAs). This starts with repositioning service management to become enterprise-focused, something we can achieve through a more outstanding education.

An end-to-end service approach

Education and examining bodies, as well as professional membership bodies, need to work together to help organisations understand that their supply and service value chains play a critical role in their success. They also need to help with strategic approaches such as SIAM and on practical methods such as outside-in thinking, where the customer journey is paramount to digital success.

Organisations, especially IT departments, often work on enhancing their element of the organisation using an inside-out view. Usually, all this does is improve their department or working area, but it does not translate as an improvement that can be felt across the enterprise, customers, consumers and partners.

Having this insight from those education and examination bodies will help organisations to establish, consider and address how service outcomes from a consumer perspective are negatively impacted by poorly thought-out or poorly joined-up commercial arrangements.

This understanding, comprehension and desire to look at services from an end-to-end perspective will be enabled as the practice of outside-in thinking will be pressed home by the education, examining and professional bodies. Latterly, this level of thinking will be implemented by those service management professionals taking this information on board and implementing it across organisational ecosystems.

Using service management to deliver an experience

We can better understand our customers' digital service perception by measuring their experience. This should not be the future of our industry, but right now I still see too many organisations measuring incorrectly; hence 'experience' measurement is our future.

An XLA (experience level agreement) is an experience metric that measures the gap between the experience you are delivering now to your employees or customers and the experience you want to provide. The concept of XLAs has been gaining traction over the last few years and is something more organisations are looking to measure.

Ultimately, our job in IT 'service' management is to look at the services we provide, measure these appropriately and continually improve them in line with the needs of our colleagues, customers and consumers. Historically, we have measured these via service levels using SLAs.

SLAs are still relevant in 2023 and possibly more so than they ever were. This is not about doing away with SLAs but more about complementing them with XLAs, so let's attempt to get on the same page about what an SLA is. The definition below is per the latest ITIL4 guidance from Axelos and PeopleCert®.

> *"A documented agreement between a service provider and a customer that identifies both services required and the expected level of service."*

An SLA is a contractual understanding between the digital IT team or vendor, the service provider and the customer about what the two parties can expect from a particular service.

SLAs are often measured through service elements that are seen as 'critical' to the delivery and success of the service. These have their label and acronym, key performance indicators (KPIs). More often than not, these critical aspects and measures are decided when a service is being designed.

A KPI is a means to measure the success or failure of these digital services and the possible penalties that might come into play if either of the two sides violates the contractual SLA.

Often, this form of measurement is deemed to be good enough to give the assumption of creating a contract between the service provider and the customer. However, this type of agreement is often misapplied. Indeed, it can no longer be relevant once a digital IT service goes live as these KPIs may no longer be as critical as they were during original discussions.

In reality, it is often the case that our SLA metrics are being met. Still, the perception of those using the service is negative. This is then used to chastise the supplier without anyone concentrating on 'why' there is negativity surrounding the service.

This goes back to our watermelon effect, where the 'green' reports do not help the IT service provider, their colleagues, customers or consumers achieve the value they had initially expected to reach while paying for the service. From the outside, everything is green. However, delve deeper, and it's all glaring red.

I cannot stress enough how often this negative aspect is left unseen or, in the context of a commercial work, left unattended or unresolved. This leads to unhappy employees and customers and eventually the loss of business to competition, possibly without us knowing why until it's too late.

There are some critical problems with SLAs, namely:

- They are no longer relevant. SLAs and KPIs are often agreed upon at a point in time. Service management professionals must work with their colleagues, customers, consumers, and partners to continually measure whether the service measures are appropriate!

As time moves on, so do the critical measures for a service.

- They are solely IT service-oriented (response, resolution, uptime, downtime, etc.); however, they don't share much information on how well or poorly the digital service performed during time periods critical to the consumers of the service.
- Most metrics used to measure the SLAs are often done at a low level; they are transactional and do not focus on looking at the service from the outside in, i.e. the consumer's perspective.
- They are, by definition, IT measures instead of organisational ones.

How you approach the 'experience' question should be built around 'value' wherever possible. If a digital service is designed well, we'll know the value we aim for. If a service is updated or redesigned, we should also seek to understand its value and co-create this with our colleagues, customers, consumers, and vendors, however appropriate. Another area to consider is our constant need for labels and acronyms.

While discussing the value, we can discuss experience in line with desired experience and service levels. These can then be agreed upon, establishing a co-created understanding of the type and value-based measures required for quality levels that customers or consumers will experience while using digital services.

It is essential that this understanding is defined in partnership and written clearly for both sides to relate correctly. This information should also be reviewed regularly and measured appropriately to ensure it remains as relevant as it was during the digital service lifecycle – never allow the measures to become outdated and irrelevant.

Ensure these measures and their review are in writing, shared and accessible. From here, we can build a clear focus on experience for the digital service with the XLA becoming the bridge between technical performance and employee/customer perception and reduce what is known as the experience gap: the gap between the experience being provided currently and the experience you want to provide as an organisation.

Experience levels should be the 'present' of IT and enterprise-focused service management. It's just a shame that not everyone has jumped on board yet.

Value-focused CoPs

Even though the concept of these communities is being understood, they are not only a tool to implement enterprise-focused service management but so much more for our industry and profession.

Using value-focused CoPs as part of an enterprise service management model promotes collaboration and communication across organisations and their ecosystems.

These communities are, in my opinion, a collaborative, valuable and – dare I say it – a modern approach for organisations looking to improve their service delivery and streamlined processes. Involving all relevant parties in the combination of enterprise service management and CoPs encourages teamwork and fosters a culture of cooperation and mutual understanding. This can lead to improved decision-making and faster resolution of issues.

In truth, no particular framework is needed; you need time and a desire to foster collaboration and empower yourself and your teams to come together and challenge one another and your leadership constructively.

You can undoubtedly leverage technology to achieve this, but only by focusing on value do you stand the best chance of aligning services with business goals, standardising procedures, promoting continual improvement, fostering collaboration, and ensuring compliance. All these things can help your organisation improve efficiency, reduce costs and enhance its reputation. These focus areas also enable you to build great teams with a mutual drive and desire to improve continually and collaborate across your enterprise and with your commercial partners.

But why stop there…

As an industry, we have several conferences per year. These include invaluable information resources and ways of working that allow knowledge and experiences to be shared.

Each of these get-togethers comes with a cost, whether that's the cost of a ticket, the cost of annual leave or billable days lost, not to mention travel, hotels, meals and the all-important coffee, tea and water.

I suggest not abandoning these events but complementing them with a series of value-focused community meetings that bring our practitioners together to discuss the topics that matter to them and share knowledge. These could be built to:

- Share experience of ways of working;
- Enable people to discuss potential career paths;
- Share feedback and tips on certification and exams;
- Build a body of knowledge;

- Feed back on what we'd like to see at more organised multi-day events;
- Discuss how we can be 'allies' to one another during challenging periods;
- Mentor and assist our colleagues; and
- Host guest speakers from the industry and organisational areas such as people and culture, finance and marketing.

These suggestions are based on feedback from my colleagues, customers and contacts in and around the industry. These would not be exhaustive and could evolve as we grow and take on members.

If you think a community such as this would be good, please email me at david@solsevenstudio.com.

Value-focused communities – service management as an ally

Value-focused CoPs aim to make a difference for those who need support in progressing and building a service management career. These, in turn, are stimulating value-focused CoPs to support groups across different IT and business areas as well to help those groups of people that benefit from allies.

Early in 2023, I had the pleasure of forming a service management community focused on demystifying service management. Our community aims to break down the barriers of entry and progression for women working in technology roles. I cannot emphasise enough how humbled I feel to be trusted to do this.

This community discusses topics that are of value to its members; these topics centre around providing opportunities to women in technology and increasing diversity and inclusion within the industry. Please join this movement at: *https://resources.reed.com/women-in-technology-mentoring-programme*.

Our first community meeting was promoted via the poster shown in Figure 16. I'd love to help you with or see your community flyers when you build your value-focused CoP. We followed this up with a community meeting that discussed an incredibly important topic: allyship.

You can see the meeting poster in Figure 17 and a link to the meeting recording in the referrals at the back of this book.

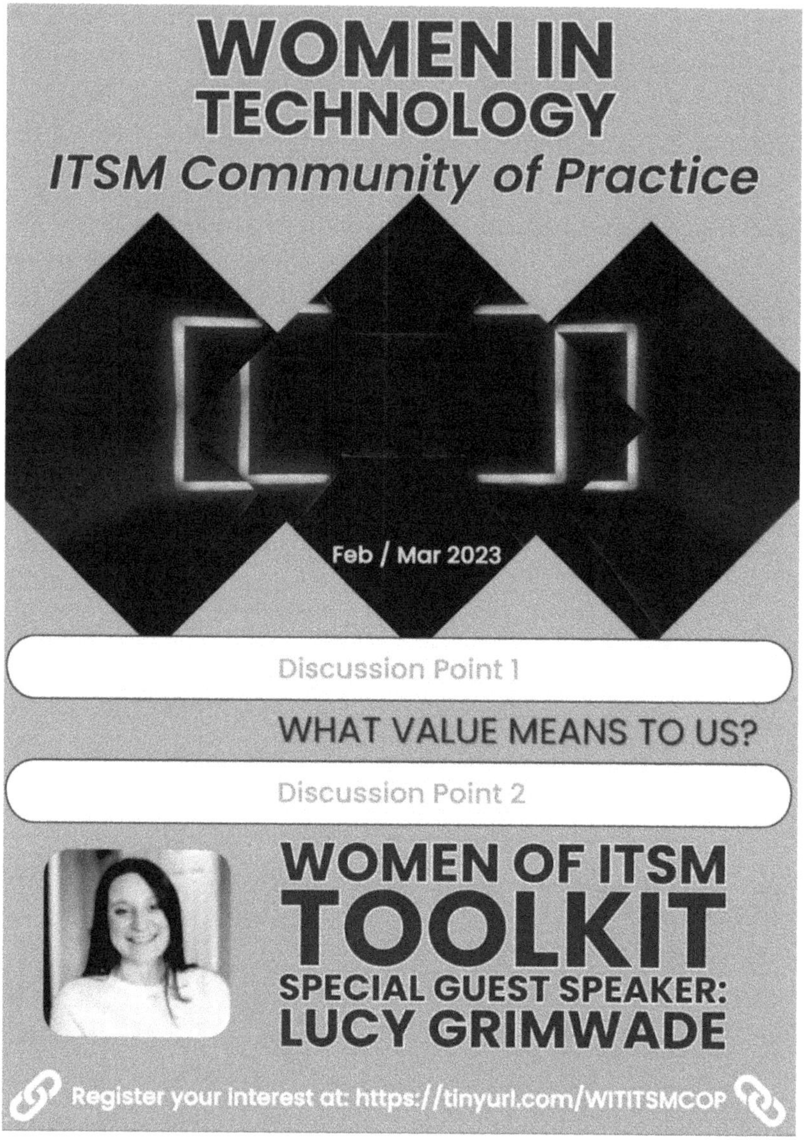

Figure 16: Women in Technology CoP Agenda

Figure 17: Women in Technology CoP Agenda

I have also been privileged to join a CoP that aims to demystify service management and help past and current members of the British Armed Forces to create a career in service management. More information can be found here: *https://www.itsmf.co.uk/armed_forces_covenant/*.

I hope that service management as a community can help other technology sectors support those that need it in progressing their lives and careers in line with their talent and enthusiasm.

Service management really can act as an ally.

Summary

What next? It's a tricky question and one I spent far too long trying to answer in this chapter.

We've discussed ITSM and how it can evolve into enterprise service management through our use of knowledge and technology, our measurement of experience and our creation of value-focused communities.

These topics are already being discussed at an international level with a view to enabling their application in the real world.

Still, as an industry of professionals, we are in danger of doing this in relative isolation.

I work on committees with the BCS, the BSI and ISO, where we discuss all things service management. I won't lie, some topics are 'drier' than others, but one thing keeps coming to me during these meetings.

Where is everyone else?

Volunteers mainly run these groups, and we have hundreds of years of experience between us. This experience is being used well, but it could be used better. We need to lift our discussions into a more expansive space; we need to invite critique and comment more suitably as engagement is low. I believe this will come from working as a community on the topics that matter to our customers, our colleagues and to you – the reader of this book.

I cannot hide my disappointment at the lack of diversity in these committees – it's not the committees' fault, and it's not intentional – but it needs fixing. We can fix this through community and empowering those of you making a career in service management to join us – regardless of your experience or certification.

We all have a voice, and we need to use it. Please share your challenges, your victories and your ideas. Please come to me and others with your ideas; we can help you realise them.

What next? I want to see fewer 'committees' and more 'communities'. I'm not sure my fellow members will agree without clarity around my statement.

Our work as committees is excellent; we make a huge difference and do so as volunteers. We spend much time reviewing documents, agreeing on standards, and getting these issued for industry use.

That difference could be further realised if we increased our inclusivity by improving our feedback loops and using communities of impactors and influencers to spread our messages.

I had just learned that these committees existed when I was 25 years into my career. Not good enough on my part but also not good enough for those working so hard within these committees to make IT and the delivery of digital services a fantastic place to work that enables organisations. This needs to be improved.

We can improve our educational entry points into service management for school leavers to corporate leaders, and we can encourage diversity and inclusivity to empower anyone to work in service management and be successful.

ITSM of the present and the future has a unique position from which it can influence whole organisations. We can use IT to deliver health care and advice where it currently does not exist, improve agricultural and supply chain efficiency through IoT, and set standards that reduce CO2 emissions.

Beyond this, we are presently discussing service management's potential impact globally and beyond. Now, more than ever, we need to strategise, design, operate and improve digital services that add value to the world.

I wish I had known all of this many years ago, and I want us to work together to build communities that can realise the potential of service management for today's world and beyond.

By taking all of these steps together, we can deliver a future state that sees service management recognised as more than just an organisational enabler but as a desirable career option that enables those within it to make a massive difference to our world.

CHAPTER 16: CONCLUSION – YOU'RE NOT ALONE

Pulling together this publication has been a challenge for me. Attempting to cover so much ground in a structured manner takes time and effort. I take my hat off to 'real' authors.

I set myself the challenge of writing *An Education in Service Management* as I'm passionate about the value service management offers as a career and the value it adds as an enterprise and organisational enabler when lifted out of focusing just on IT. I hope that passion is evident, and I hope you've found the book to be an education in service management.

I have sought to highlight the importance of having a child-like curiosity, a willingness to listen and an ability to communicate as being core skills of a service management professional. Writing this book in isolation has set me off on various paths of discussion, giving me a platform to communicate my thoughts, and all without the ability to communicate and seek feedback as I write.

As somebody who has written hundreds of processes and reports, I still do not consider myself a 'natural' writer, yet I find myself trying to explain something important to me as both a profession and a practice.

I sincerely hope that I've met the objectives you set when choosing to read this book and that I've answered the questions and discussion points raised when we began this journey. I hope I have left you with enough input to set you off on your path to building your service management career and delivered a guide to using enterprise-focused service management to enable your organisation, its customers, consumers and partners.

My overriding objectives were to demystify service management and to discuss how you can build a career in it that is focused on creating value for our customers, though not simply a value based on finance or other quantifiable measures. A career that is stimulating, challenging, rewarding and one that you can be proud of, and that you can explain to those around you!

I was also seeking to go beyond those values that are seemingly quantifiable and provide you as a professional or as a leader with a set of practices that positively influence the overall performance of your digital teams and your organisation, delivering tangible benefits to your customers. Practices and ways of working designed to co-create values that build an experience that delights the customers of your digital services and to innovate your digital service offerings.

By focusing on these values, we can empower and entrust your digital service teams to get ahead of the curve in identifying service fragility and work together to continually evolve and develop your organisation's service strategy, products and service offerings in what is an ever-changing world.

We've covered much ground together, and I hope this is just the beginning.

To return to the origins of our discussion.

You're not alone

I want to emphasise this as I hope reading of this book has made you realise that not only are other people asking the questions you have been asking, but they are also living through these questions in the real world. It's not just you.

This does not need to be the end of our relationship; we can still write new pages together. I'm about to repeat myself from an earlier chapter of the book, but I think it's worth reiterating.

The challenges we face today, in or out of work, will have been met and conquered by others. If service management has taught me one thing, it is that we can learn more from looking at the past than we can by simply sitting and wondering about our future... We make our future through a mixture of judgement based on experience, judgement based on our gut feeling and no small amount of luck.

After reading this book, I hope you agree with this statement. We can learn so much from one another; we don't need to be in the same office or organisation to do so; technology makes the world a small place, and we need to adapt our working methods to this.

We can improve our probability of success in our careers, lives and across enterprises globally by sharing our thoughts, experiences, failures and successes. For me, that is the true purpose of book – sharing and improving on a continual and iterative basis.

To reiterate, you're not alone. You may benefit from joining a membership organisation that specialises in our fields of expertise, if you have not already done so. I am a member of the BCS and the itSMF UK. These membership groups offer helpful advice via their web pages and events. I've built a great network since I joined. I wish I'd done so sooner, as meeting like-minded professionals opened my eyes to the challenges we all face, professionally and personally.

- BCS membership: *https://www.bcs.org/membership-and-registrations/become-a-member/*.
- itSMF UK membership: *https://www.itsmf.co.uk/services/membership/*.

For those outside the UK, please go to the itSMF International page below to find your local membership: *https://www.itsmfi.org/page/ContactInformation*.

It's good to talk. If I cannot help, my network probably has someone who can help you. We can work together to solve complex issues or offer helpful suggestions. And, of course, if you need to speak, share, or vent, I am here to help – on absolutely anything service management-related or otherwise.

If you need an ally, I'd like to be that ally. I may not have all the answers, but I can provide a good ear, and I'd be hopeful of offering advice to get you where you need to be.

In addition, I can offer you access to a newly formed CoP that will be available to help you. As a community, the ITSM People (*https://www.itsmpeople.co.uk*) and I will be working together to create a new ITSM-focused CoP. This will be labelled as a CoP for ITSM People by The ITSM People.

I will act as the initial chair for this community and would love it if you could join us; we intend to build upon those topics enclosed in this book and so much more. It would be great to have you there.

And so, to reiterate a point one final time, we cannot stop here. We must continually improve, help, and act as allies to one another and our customers, consumers and partners. I hope we one day look back on this book as just another example of 'learning, unlearning and relearning' and connecting as a community.

You're not alone.

Thanks for reading.

Kindest regards,

David Barrow CITP FBCS
November 2023

APPENDIX: RESOURCES

Links to service management resources:

- **AGILE**: *https://www.exin.com/agile-devops-lean/exin-agile-scrum/exin-agile-scrum-foundation/*.
- **Astride assessment tool**: *https://www.exin.com/astride-by-exin/*.
- **Axelos**: *https://www.axelos.com/*.
- **British Computer Society (BCS)**: *https://www.bcs.org/*.
- **British Computer Society membership**: *https://www.bcs.org/membership-and-registrations/become-a-member/*.
- **ChatGPT**: (*https://chat.openai.com/auth/login*) grants you a worldwide, royalty-free, non-exclusive licence to use, copy, modify and distribute the text generated for any lawful purpose. It is always a good practice to give appropriate credit to the source of information used in your work.
- **COBIT**: *https://www.isaca.org/resources/cobit*.
  ***Co-Creating Value in Organizations with ITIL 4*, by David Barrow:**
  https://www.tsoshop.co.uk/product/9780113318513/Business-and-Management/IT-service-management/Co-creating-value-in-organizations-with-ITIL-4-a-guide-for-consultants-executives-and-managers/.

- **DevOps**: *https://www.exin.com/agile-devops-lean/exin-devops/exin-devops-foundation/*.
- **EXIN**: *https://www.exin.com/*.
- **EXIN career paths**: *https://www.exin.com/career-paths/*.
- **ISO/IEC 20000**: *https://www.iso.org/standard/70636.html*.
- **IT4IT**: *https://www.opengroup.org/it4it*.
- **itSMF UK:** *https://www.itsmf.co.uk/services/membership/*.
- **Lean**: *https://www.exin.com/agile-devops-lean/exin-lean-it/exin-lean-it-foundation/*.
- **Lean Six Sigma:** *https://www.exin.com/agile-devops-lean/exin-lssa-lean-six-sigma/*.
- **PRINCE2**: *https://www.prince2.com/uk/what-is-prince2*.
- **SIAM:** *https://www.scopism.com/*.
- **SIAM Body of Knowledges:** *https://www.itgovernancepublishing.co.uk/product/service-integration-and-management-siam-foundation-body-of-knowledge-bok-second-edition*, *https://www.itgovernancepublishing.co.uk/product/service-integration-and-management-siam-professional-body-of-knowledge-bok-second-edition*.
- **Skills Framework for the Information Age (SFIA)**: *https://sfia-online.org/en*.
- **Top tips from service management experts**: *https://itsmf.cz/wp/wp-*

content/uploads/2023/07/IT_Governance-Tips-from-ITSM-experts-v1.1.pdf.
- **USM method**: *https://usm-portal.com*.
- **VeriSM**: *https://verism.global/*.
- **"What is SIAM?", by Claire Agutter:** *https://www.scopism.com/what-is-service-integration-and-management-siam/*.

Links to Book Research and Referral

- **A Giant Web Of Submarine Cables Connects India To The Internet And World:** *https://www.indiatimes.com/technology/news/submarine-cable-network-india-internet-link-world-537327.html*.
- **How the Internet extends across the sea floor:** *https://www.sacyr.com/en/-/asi-se-extiende-internet-por-el-fondo-del-mar*.
- **Why Being A Jack Of All Trades Is Essential For Success:** *https://www.forbes.com/sites/jodiecook/2021/05/13/why-being-a-jack-of-all-trades-is-essential-for-success/*.
- **2023 ManageEngine White Paper: Service Management Strategies for the next 3 years from 10 ITSM experts & leaders:** *https://www.manageengine.com/products/service-desk/itsm/service-management-strategy.html*.

Mentoring programmes and links

- **Reed Women in Technology Mentoring Programme**

https://resources.reed.com/women-in-technology-mentoring-programme.

- **British Computer Society mentoring:** *https://www.bcs.org/membership-and-registrations/become-a-member/mentoring/*.

Service management communities of practice

- **Women in Technology ITSM CoP:** *https://resources.reed.com/women-in-technology-mentoring-programme*.
- **Women in Technology ITSM CoP:** *"All you ever wanted to know about Allyship…but never dared to ask"*, *https://youtu.be/c9FPc1QsGrA*.
- **The Open Service Community** *https://openservicecommunity.com/*.
- **The Scopism SIAM Community** *https://scopism.circle.so/home*.
- **itSMF UK Armed Forces CoP**: *https://www.itsmf.co.uk/armed_forces_covenant*.
- **The ITSM People CoP**: *https://www.itsmpeople.co.uk*.

British computer society designations

- **BCS Professional membership (MBCS)**: If you're a skilled, ethical IT professional looking to raise your profile and career potential, join the BCS as a professional member. *https://www.bcs.org/membership-and-registrations/become-a-member/professional-membership/*.

- **BSC Chartered Information Technology Professional (CITP)**: Chartered IT Professional is the independent standard of competence and professionalism in the technology industry. *https://www.bcs.org/membership-and-registrations/get-registered/chartered-it-professional/*.
- **BCS Fellowship:** BCS Fellowship is home to the most influential professionals in the digital industry. Connect with the leaders who share your passion for technology, technical expertise, business acumen, ethics and social responsibilities. *https://www.bcs.org/membership-and-registrations/become-a-member/bcs-fellowship/*.
- **itSMF UK Membership** *https://www.itsmf.co.uk/services/membership/*.
- **itSMF Global Membership** The ITSMF has global chapters, you can find the chapter and all relevant contact details here: *https://www.itsmfi.org/page/ContactInformation*.

Recommended podcasts/YouTube channels

- **The ITSM Crowd,** *https://www.youtube.com/@TheITSMCrowd/featured*.
- **The Enterprise Digital Podcast** *https://enterprisedigitalpodcast.com/*.
- **Service Management Leadership Podcast** *https://servicemanagement.us/media-appearances-2/*.
- **Reed Career Q&As – Technology Role Models:**

https://www.youtube.com/@technologyrolemodels-diver7009.

- **IT's all about choices:** *https://www.youtube.com/@ITsallaboutchoices./streams.*

FURTHER READING

IT Governance Publishing (ITGP) is the world's leading publisher for governance and compliance. Our industry-leading pocket guides, books, training resources and toolkits are written by real-world practitioners and thought leaders. They are used globally by audiences of all levels, from students to C-suite executives.

Our high-quality publications cover all IT governance, risk and compliance frameworks and are available in a range of formats. This ensures our customers can access the information they need in the way they need it.

Our other publications about service management include:

- *ITIL® 4 Essentials – Your essential guide for the ITIL 4 Foundation exam and beyond, second edition* by Claire Agutter, *www.itgovernancepublishing.co.uk/product/itil-4-essentials-your-essential-guide-for-the-itil-4-foundation-exam-and-beyond-second-edition*
- *Service Integration and Management (SIAM™) Foundation Body of Knowledge (BoK), Second edition* by Claire Agutter et al., *https://www.itgovernancepublishing.co.uk/product/service-integration-and-management-siam-foundation-body-of-knowledge-bok-second-edition*
- *Service Integration and Management (SIAM™) Professional Body of Knowledge (BoK), Second edition,* Michelle Major-Goldsmith, Simon Dorst,

Claire Agutter et al., *https://www.itgovernancepublishing.co.uk/product/service-integration-and-management-siam-professional-body-of-knowledge-bok-second-edition*

For more information on ITGP and branded publishing services, and to view our full list of publications, visit *www.itgovernancepublishing.co.uk*.

To receive regular updates from ITGP, including information on new publications in your area(s) of interest, sign up for our newsletter at *www.itgovernancepublishing.co.uk/topic/newsletter*.

Branded publishing

Through our branded publishing service, you can customise ITGP publications with your company's branding.

Find out more at

www.itgovernancepublishing.co.uk/topic/branded-publishing-services.

Related services

ITGP is part of GRC International Group, which offers a comprehensive range of complementary products and services to help organisations meet their objectives.

For a full range of resources on ITIL visit *www.itgovernance.co.uk/shop/category/itil*.

Training services

The IT Governance training programme is built on our extensive practical experience designing and implementing management systems based on ISO standards, best practice and regulations.

Our courses help attendees develop practical skills and comply with contractual and regulatory requirements. They also support career development via recognised qualifications.

Learn more about our training courses in ITIL and view the full course catalogue at *www.itgovernance.co.uk/training*.

Professional services and consultancy

We are a leading global consultancy of IT governance, risk management and compliance solutions. We advise businesses around the world on their most critical issues and present cost-saving and risk-reducing solutions based on international best practice and frameworks.

We offer a wide range of delivery methods to suit all budgets, timescales and preferred project approaches.

Find out how our consultancy services can help your organisation at *www.itgovernance.co.uk/consulting*.

Industry news

Want to stay up to date with the latest developments and resources in the IT governance and compliance market? Subscribe to our Security Spotlight newsletter and we will send you mobile-friendly emails with fresh news and features about your preferred areas of interest, as well as unmissable offers and free resources to help you successfully start your projects. *www.itgovernance.co.uk/security-spotlight-newsletter*

EU for product safety is Stephen Evans, The Mill Enterprise Hub, Stagreenan, Drogheda, Co. Louth, A92 CD3D, Ireland. (servicecentre@itgovernance.eu)

www.ingramcontent.com/pod-product-compliance
Lightning Source LLC
LaVergne TN
LVHW051043210926
848486LV00001B/4
9781787785618